A LEVEL
Questions and Answers

ENGLISH

Ian Barr & Chris Walton

SERIES EDITORS:

Letts
EDUCATIONAL

Every effort has been made to trace copyright holders and to obtain their permission for the use of copyright material. The authors and publishers will gladly receive any information enabling them to rectify any error or omission in subsequent editions.

First published 1995
Reprinted 1995, 1999 twice,
Letts Educational
Aldine Place
London W12 8AW
Tel: 0208-743 7514
Fax :0208-743 8451
E-mail:mail@lettsed.co.uk

British Library Cataloguing in Publication Data

A CIP record for this book is available from the British Library.

ISBN 1 85758 354 X

Questions

Tasks 8 and 9 (Unit 5): Reproduced by kind permission of the Associated Examining Board. Any answers or hints on answers are the sole responsibility of the authors and have not been provided or approved by the Board. Tasks 3, 4, 10, 11, 13, 14 and 21 (Unit 5): Reproduced by permission of the University of Cambridge Local Examinations Syndicate. The University of Cambridge Local Examinations Syndicate bears no responsibility for the example answers to questions taken from its past question papers which are contained in this publication. Tasks 5, 6, 7, 19 and 20 (Unit 5): Reproduced by kind permission of the Northern Examinations and Assessment Board. The authors accept responsibility for answers provided, which may not necessarily constitute the only possible solutions. Tasks 1, 2, 15, 16, 17 and 18 (Unit 5): Reproduced by kind permission of the University of Oxford Delegacy of Local Examinations.

Extracts

pp18–19 'Snakecharmer' reprinted from *The Colossus and Other Poems* by Sylvia Plath, published by Faber and Faber Ltd. Reprinted with permission; pp19–20 'In the Snake Park' reprinted from *Collected Poems* by William Plomer, published by Jonathan Cape, reprinted by permission of Jonathan Cape; pp23–24 'After Apple-picking' reprinted from *The Poetry of Robert Frost*, edited by Edward Connery Lathem, published by Jonathan Cape, reprinted by kind permission of the Estate of Robert Frost and Jonathan Cape; pp24–25 'Apples' by Laurie Lee, from *Selected Poems* by Laurie Lee, published by Penguin, reprinted by permission of the Peters Fraser & Dunlop Group Ltd; pp27–29 'Rhapsody on a Windy Night' reprinted from *Collected Poems 1909-1962*, by T S Eliot, published by Faber and Faber Ltd. Reprinted with permission; pp33–34 'Wind' reprinted from *The Hawk in the Rain*, by Ted Hughes, published by Faber and Faber Ltd. Reprinted with permission; p42 from *Brighton Rock* by Graham Greene, published by Heinemann, reprinted by permission of David Higham Associates; p45 from *The Heart of the Matter* by Graham Greene, published by Heinemann, reprinted by permission of David Higham Associates; pp45–46 from *The Levant Trilogy* by Olivia Manning, published by Weidenfeld & Nicolson, reprinted by permission of the Orion Publishing Group Ltd; pp68–69 from *A Man for All Seasons*, by Robert Bolt, published by Heinemann Publishers (Oxford) Ltd. Reprinted with permission; pp74–75 from *Wide Sargasso Sea* by Jean Rhys (Penguin Books 1968, first published by Andre Deutsch), copyright © Jean Rhys 1966, reprinted by permission of Penguin Books; p76 'Ritornello' copyright © Charles Tomlinson 1985, reprinted from Charles Tomlinson's *Collected Poems* (1985) by permission of Oxford University Press. pp76–77 'Out of Danger' from *Out of Danger* by James Fenton, published by Penguin, reprinted by permission of the Peters Fraser & Dunlop Group Ltd; pp77–78 from *A Voyage Round my Father* by John Mortimer, published by Methuen, reprinted by permission of the Peters Fraser & Dunlop Group Ltd; pp79–80 from *Hotel du Lac* by Anita Brookner, copyright © Anita Brookner. Reprinted with permission; p82 'Disgrace' reprinted from *Mean Time*, by Carol Ann Duffy, published by Anvil Press Poetry, 1993. Reprinted with permission; p83 from *City of the Mind* by Penelope Lively (Penguin Books 1992, first published by Andre Deutsch), copyright © Penelope Lively 1992, reprinted by permission of Penguin Books; pp83–84 from *Hawksmoor* by Peter Ackroyd (Hamish Hamilton, 1985), copyright © Peter Ackroyd, 1985, reprinted by permission of Hamish Hamilton Ltd; pp84–85 'Carousel' reprinted from *Wailing the Dead to Sleep*, by Lucinda Roy, published by Bogle L'Ouverture Press. Reprinted with permission; pp86–87 from 'The Function of Criticism' reprinted from *Selected Essays* by T S Eliot, published by Faber and Faber Ltd. Reprinted with permission; p88 from *The Jewel in the Crown*, by Paul Scott, published by Heinemann, reprinted by permission of David Higham Associates; p90 from 'That in Aleppo Once' reprinted from *Nabokov's Dozen*, by Vladimir Nabokov, published by Weidenfeld & Nicolson, reprinted by permission of the Orion Publishing Group Ltd; p91 'The Man in Black' reprinted from *The Colossus and Other Poems* by Sylvia Plath, published by Faber and Faber Ltd. Reprinted with permission; pp97–98 from *Howards End* by E M Forster, reprinted by permission of King's College, Cambridge, and The Society of Authors as the literary representatives of the E M Forster Estate; pp99–101 from *The Caretaker* by Harold Pinter, published by Faber and Faber Ltd. Reprinted with permission; pp101–103 from *Waiting for Godot* by Samuel Beckett, published by Faber and Faber Ltd. Reprinted with permission; pp103–104 'Red Hills of Home' by Chenjerai Hove, reprinted by permission of Mambo Press; pp106–108 from *Next Time I'll Sing to You* by James Saunders, published by Heinemann Educational, 1986, reprinted by permission of Andre Deutsch Ltd.

Printed in Great Britain by Ashford Colour Press

Letts Educational is the trading name of BPP (Letts Educational) Ltd

Contents

THE IMPORTANCE OF USING QUESTIONS FOR REVISION

Past examination questions can play a major part in revising for examinations. It is important not to start practising questions too early, however. Nothing can be more disheartening than trying to attempt a question which you do not understand because you have not mastered the topic. Therefore, study a topic thoroughly before attempting any questions on it.

How can past examination questions help you to prepare for the examination? It is unlikely that any question you attempt will appear in exactly the same form on the papers you are going to take. However, the examiner is restricted on what can be set, as questions must cover the whole syllabus and test certain Assessment Objectives. The number of totally original questions that can be set on any part of the syllabus is very limited and so similar ideas occur over and over again. It certainly will help you if the question you are trying to answer in an examination is familiar and you know you have attempted similar questions before. This is a great boost for your confidence — and confidence is all-important for examination success.

Practising examination questions will also highlight gaps in your knowledge and understanding which you can then go back and revise more thoroughly. Attempting past questions will get you used to the type of language used in examination questions.

Finally, having access to answers, as you do in this book, will enable you to see clearly what is required by the examiner, how best to answer each question, and the amount of detail required. Attention to detail is a key aspect of achieving success at A level.

MAXIMISING YOUR MARKS

One of the keys to examination success is to know how marks are gained and lost by candidates. There are two important aspects to this: ensuring you follow the instructions (or 'rubric') on the examination paper and understanding how papers are marked by examiners.

Often candidates fail to gain the marks they deserve because they do not follow the rubric exactly. Follow the advice on p13 of this book carefully. It explains the terms and instructions used in the rubrics of English Literature examinations.

Mark schemes in English Literature describe the sort of assessment objectives and qualities that candidates are expected to display in their answers. Examiners read the answers carefully and then have to make a judgement in order to use the mark band that best fits the qualities of the answer. They literally ask themselves questions such as: how well has this candidate met the objectives? Has the candidate covered enough of the objectives for a particular mark band? Have the objectives been met with ease, with an appropriate style of writing? What is missing? Obviously, therefore, it is worth knowing what is expected of you.

Examiners think and mark positively. They never start by trying to find what you have *not* included: they mark what they read. So be positive with your answers; organise points methodically; make a range of points; develop points of interpretation. It is possible to raise your marks into higher bands by helping the examiner follow your ideas. Good planning and sound organisation always produce better essays.

HOW TO USE THIS BOOK

Q & A English is the perfect companion for practising the type of questions you will be given in your A-Level English Literature examination.

This book deals only with unprepared passages of prose, and 'unseen' poetry. It is not intended to give you guidance on the preparation you need for set texts, nor for English Language examinations. However, you will find that most of the skills of critical appreciation are transferable, especially to the essays you write on set texts. Really, the more you are capable of understanding what is required for critical appreciation, the easier it will be to construct answers on your set texts. Essentially, the skills are the same.

In Unit 1, the revision summary, you will find advice on how to approach questions on unprepared passages, followed by revision of a large number of the literary terms that you may need to know.

Units 2–4 present for appreciation passages of **poetry**, **prose**, and **drama** (including some which ask for a comparison), along with essays that have been written in response to the passages. Accompanying each text and essay is an examiner's commentary on the nature of the critical tasks set in the questions, and on the strengths of the answers. If you want a real challenge, why not use these passages to attempt your own answers, in addition to the exam questions set in the Practice Section (Unit 5, pp.74–115)? There is a full range of answer types. In what we consider to be the reader's best interests, the essays have been tidied up slightly in terms of grammar and spelling. They have all been chosen as good examples of their type, although they are by no means perfect.

Unit 5 provides a range of passages and questions for exam practice, many from actual specimen papers published by the various Examination Boards. This will give you the opportunity to practise the questions as you prepare for your exam.

THE CORE FOR ENGLISH LITERATURE

At the end of your course you will be taking an Advanced Level examination set by one of the GCE Boards.

Some time ago, concern was expressed that there was no real control over examination syllabuses, with the result that there was no guarantee that all students would arrive in institutions of higher education with the same skills and knowledge, even when they notionally had the same qualification. The same problem existed for employers.

Accordingly, work has started on establishing cores for all A Level subjects. It was intended that the cores would define knowledge and understanding and the skills which were to be covered by all syllabuses of the same nature. Common assessment objectives would also be defined.

It was decided that three cores would be established to cover English and English Literature which would reflect the different styles of syllabus already in existence. They would be entitled English Language, English Literature, and English Language and Literature. As this book concentrates on critical appreciation of literature, the English Literature core is the most relevant, and is examined in detail on the next page.

The cores also apply to Advanced Supplementary examinations. Although there is only half the content, and although they use half the study time of Advanced Level examinations, they are nevertheless at the same standard.

It is important to remember that the core is not the syllabus — it is a framework in which the details of the syllabus are then developed.

English Literature

The core for English Literature starts from an extremely concrete base, in that it specifies the nature of texts which must form a basis of study: one Shakespeare play must be studied; one prose work; one work of poetry (although this is not defined and is clearly open to different interpretations by the Examining Boards); one work of drama. It is important to remember that this is a minimum requirement and syllabuses generally require broader study.

What is essential is that a range of texts is studied and that the range covers historical periods from 1370 on, as well as types of texts. The core as published also contains the phrase 'be of sufficient substance and quality to merit serious consideration at advanced level'. Although this phrase would be interpreted differently in debate, it would seem to mean substantial texts from the canon of English literature.

When you start an advanced level of study of English Literature, the first skills to develop are those which determine the necessary approach and the ways in which literary study can be carried out. So it is important to look at how writers shape their work in terms of the form, the detail of structure and the language in which their writing is expressed. In doing so, you will discover different levels of meaning in texts and discover that writing can be interpreted in a variety of ways. It is rarely possible to state that one interpretation is correct rather than another. The ability to fit a text to its historical period and to a particular literary movement is a necessary skill to aid interpretation.

Other skills are associated with personal response and reaction to literary texts. Understanding should result in a response to both explicit and implicit meanings; students must be able not only to describe but to make judgements about features which are observed; depth of study should allow an understanding and interpretation of the attitudes and values of the writer. Ultimately, the response may be personal and unique to the student, but it must be based closely on what is read. Finally, the fundamental skill of possessing the ability to express understanding, views and judgements in fluent and sophisticated writing must continue to be developed.

Again, the assessment objectives follow logically from this base of knowledge and skills. 'Candidates will be required to demonstrate:

(a) an ability to respond with understanding to texts of different types and periods;

(b) an understanding of the ways in which writers' choices of form, structure and language express meanings;

(c) knowledge of the contexts in which literary works are written and understood;

(d) an ability to discuss their own and other readers' interpretations of texts;

(e) an ability to produce informed, independent opinions and judgements;

(f) an ability to communicate clearly the knowledge, understanding and insight appropriate to literary study.'

CRITICAL APPRECIATION OF UNPREPARED POETRY AND PROSE

In A Level English Literature exams, one of the ways in which you are examined is through the use of **unprepared passages of poetry and prose**. Put simply, this means that you are required to undertake skills of reading, comprehension, interpretation and writing, in a limited period of time, in response to poems or prose extracts which you have (unless by chance) not met before. You may also be asked to compare passages or poems. These texts are usually connected by theme or content.

This is quite a demanding set of tasks and skills, and you need to be well prepared to tackle them by the end of your A Level course, because the questions are weighted quite heavily in terms of the proportions of marks allocated. This is because the unprepared critical appreciation (which used to be called practical criticism) is seen as an independent assessment of your skills of understanding and criticising literary texts.

Before you start to look at the examples of questions and answers (passages of prose, drama or poetry, followed by exam questions and then students' answers), there is a consideration of the skills required, and also, pp.7–12, there is a revision summary of the literary and linguistic techniques which you will need to know and apply to texts that you are writing about in the exam. The skills are set out for you in this chapter as a series of answers to questions — we hope they are the kinds of questions which you might want to have answered.

What is meant by 'close reading'?

Clearly, arriving at an A Level English Literature examination, you will know that reading must be analytical and must give you the chance to interpret meanings and ideas. You will have done this repeatedly in your study of whole texts, both poetry and prose. Yet it is sometimes easy to forget this need for analysis and interpretation when faced with a new passage in an exam. It is important, especially in the second and third readings of the passage, that you look well beyond the subject matter or content. As quickly as possible, you need to recognise such features as: meanings (including deeper layers of meaning), feelings, emotional forces, moods, atmospheres and tones, connections, relationships between one part of the text and another, the writers' attitudes to their subject matter and themes. In addition to these, you will also be expected to show how the use of language — the poetic or literary techniques, the form and style — contributes to the meanings and effects.

You need to read the passages two or three times at least, and make some notes on them. It is a good idea to underline sections that strike you as important, and make comments in the margin to explain points and draw your attention to poetic or literary techniques.

Above all, a close reading should help you notice features beyond the literal level: you must use the reading time to recognise the meanings that lie behind the language.

What should be expressed in my answer?

Most questions draw your attention to particular features in the texts, e.g. characterisation, irony, narrative, mood. This will provide you with a useful point of focus. It is rare, but not impossible, to be given a completely open task, such as 'Write a critical appreciation of the following poem or passage'. Assuming that you are asked to concentrate on specific features, it is very important that you attend to these in your approach, although you may of course also wish to refer to other elements of the text.

All the examination boards are looking for roughly the same skills, and any differences between them are either marginal, or simply different in emphasis, or in the wording used in objectives and mark schemes. To summarise the skills you need, we reproduce here extracts from the publications of two examination boards. The first list is that of the Associated Examining Board's assessment objectives relevant to the examination of unprepared poetry and prose.

The examination will assess a candidate's ability to:

- respond with understanding to texts of different types and periods;
- understand the ways in which writers' choices of form, structure and language express meanings;
- discuss their own and other readers' interpretations of texts;
- produce informed, independent opinions and judgements;
- communicate clearly the knowledge, understanding and insight appropriate to literary study;
- explore layers of meanings in texts;
- appreciate features of texts such as character, argument and imagery;
- show how texts may excite emotions in readers or audiences;
- make meaningful connections between texts (this will only apply to unprepared passages if a comparison is requested).

(The AEB refers to other objectives, but these are designed to be met in your study of prepared texts.)

The second extract is from The University of Oxford Delegacy of Local Examinations' mark scheme for the Critical Appraisal questions. This extract will be more useful to you, in that it informs you what you actually have to achieve in your answers. The Oxford Board looks to reward evidence of:

- careful analysis of content and expression;
- independent opinion and evaluation, when this is supported by evidence from the text;
- awareness, where appropriate, of audience and purpose;
- awareness of context, including period conditions, characteristics, style and vocabulary;
- awareness of the characteristics and exigencies (needs) of genre and form;
- sensitivity to the use of language: vocabulary, tone, nuance, implication, ambiguity;
- knowledgeable use (as opposed to mere display) of critical terms;
- clarity, precision and felicity (a good choice) of expression.

What is the correct balance between discussing content and style or form?

It is best not to think in terms of a balance in this respect, but to remember instead that all works of literature are created by the use of language. Anything that you discuss in terms of content — the meanings, messages, attitudes, moods or themes — relies on the style and form of the language: it is not possible to separate the two. At this level of examination, you must always be trying to explain not just what a text is about, but how its meanings have been arranged by the writer.

So, what is a good critical appreciation going to be like?

In view of the inter-dependence of content, style and form, you should think along the following lines as you approach your exam: there are three kinds of essays which are not really acceptable, or at least, they are not likely to gain high marks! The first deals only with the content, with no reference to the way the text has been created; the second, equally inadequate, covers only the language and never considers meaning; the third may appear on the surface to be acceptable, but when you think about it, is also inadequate. This is the sort of essay in which there is reference to content and meaning, and a *display* of knowledge of features of language, but which fails to connect the two.

As you read through this book, try to identify those essays in which candidates have been able to handle content along with style and form as a whole task or unit. These candidates will have recognised that literature is a construction, or an artefact, and that the meanings are embedded in the language.

'To handle content along with style and form as a whole task or unit' — what does this mean in practice?

It is a good idea to go into your examination with some 'dos' and 'don'ts' in mind. The trick is never to separate the language techniques as if you were reading a catalogue or spotting trains! Here are a few examples:

Instead of: 'The rhyming pattern is regular . . .', how about 'The regular rhyming pattern contributes to the theme of . . .'

Instead of: 'The poet uses a lot of alliteration. There is an example of this in the third line', consider 'The frequent alliteration stresses the poet's attitudes. For example, the sounds in the third line express the mood of . . .'

Never simply : 'The form of the poem is a sonnet', but preferably: 'The conventional sonnet form is appropriate here to the theme of the uncertain future of human life'.

How important is my own expression?

Very! Just as we cannot separate content or meaning from style and form, neither can there be a distinction between the ideas and arguments of your essays, and the means by which you express them. Please remember that the conventions of a literary essay require you to write in a formal and organised manner, and the more you can plan your points prior to writing, the easier it will be to achieve this.

There is no one model of a good answer: you will need to practise in order to find the style that seems to suit you best, and it is important to become increasingly confident in this style of writing as you approach your examination. There are, however, certain key principles and skills which your style and organisation must involve. Again, all the examination boards are looking to credit roughly the same qualities (and incidentally, remember that examiners are delighted to read work which is interesting to read through the quality of its expression). We publish here an extract from the University of London Examinations and Assessment Council's Marking Profile for candidates' answers. To award the higher marks in their range, examiners with London University take into account the following:

- in terms of the relevance of the answer: essays must be full; they will note subtlety, complexities and possible disagreements; there will have been discussion;
- the content will be full, relevant and incisive (focused — the opposite of waffle!) with sufficient and apt example;
- the structure must be progressive, pertinent, focused, convincing and well put together;
- finally, in terms of style and technical accuracy, London University seeks to award marks to candidates who are clear, incisive, even elegant, and accurate.

If there are two passages for comparison, do I have to state a preference?

Sometimes you are asked to state which of two poems or passages of prose you prefer. Clearly, if required to do so, you must make a judgement. Sometimes you are told that you do not have to state a preference, but you may do so if you wish. In this case, make a judgement if one occurs to you, but if both texts appear to have an equal effect or impact on you, then it may be best to avoid a preference — after all, why should you prefer the work of one writer over that of another?

If you are stating a preference, the important thing to do is to argue the reasons for your choice, and to make sure that the reasons, and your expression of them, are relevant. Many candidates trip up with this part of their answer. They all too readily forget that they should still be displaying the skills of appreciation, just as much as in the main part of their essay. The relevance of a comparison usually lies in the candidate's ability to argue which writer has been more successful in achieving an effect — perhaps in creating a memorable or dramatic scene, in establishing a character, or in the evocation of a mood. Remember that a statement of preference should not be a simple assertion; it is pointless saying what you prefer, unless you can say why.

At its worst, this type of question can lead to utter irrelevance. We have answers containing such

phrases as: 'I prefer the first poem because I found it easier to understand . . .', or 'The first passage is better because it was written in the twentieth century and is therefore easier to relate to . . .'!

The best answers will be phrased in much more relevant ways, e.g.: 'The striking imagery of the first poem creates a more vivid impression of the scene . . .', or 'The second extract is more successful because the ideas are there more by implication, whereas the first writer is more inclined to preach to the reader . . .'.

Is there anything else I can do to prepare for this exam?

Preparation for this part of your exam cannot ever be exact. Obviously, you will not be able to prepare an informed response to the texts in the same way that you can for your set books. However, you can, and should, be prepared to read more widely during your course. This will make you familiar with different kinds of texts, and their varied styles and purposes. It is also a good idea to read poetry for pleasure, to get the feel of the many different responses that poets can evoke, and to be familiar with that difficult skill of trying to unravel, or deconstruct, the language and meanings of obscure poems. Below you will find a glossary of the more important literary terms, which we advise you to know — but only to use, as suggested above, in context.

Finally, try to practise the conventions of a literary essay. Place inverted commas around quotations; isolate whole quotations on separate lines; if you are using the title, underline it; refer only to the writer's surname, and certainly never the Christian name only; avoid waffle or prevarication, especially in introductions (e.g. 'After reading this poem a few times we can clearly see that it takes as its subject matter . . .'); avoid childish personal response ('I really can respond to this poem; it's just the sort of poem I like!'); credit the poet with the constructions ('he suggests', or 'she registers the mood', never 'it says in the final verse')!

GLOSSARY OF USEFUL LITERARY TERMS

You have already been reminded that when you refer to literary techniques, you must do so in context. There are a number of technical, literary or poetic terms which you can be expected to know and use with confidence at A Level. Our experience is that weaker candidates either use them with a lack of confidence, or 'spot' them in the texts, without really being able to discuss their effects. It is a good idea to practise using technical terms during your study of set texts on the course, and to remind yourself of them before you sit your critical appreciation exam. Here is a list of the terms you are most likely to need.

allegory: a work of literature which stands for something else, other than the meanings in its own subject matter. In a sense, an allegory is like an extended metaphor, an image being contrasted with other ideas. There are recurrent themes in allegorical poems — love and religion common amongst them. One of the most celebrated examples of allegory is John Bunyan's *The Pilgrim's Progress* (1678) in which the central character, Christian, disillusioned with the ways of the world, sets out on a journey to find heaven. His worldly journey is an allegory of his quest for an understanding of the truth about real Christianity. (Journeys are a popular form for allegorical works. As readers we have to 'suspend our disbelief' and accept that the events on the journey, and the make-believe characters Christian meets, stand for other messages and ideas.)

alliteration: repetition of consonants, commonly used in poetry, to create an effect associated with meaning. An example from *The Rape of the Lock*, by Alexander Pope:

> 'He spoke; the spirits from the sails descend'

allusion: references to other works or cultures in either prose or poetry. Chaucer, for example, included many classical and Biblical allusions in his poetry, as did Hardy in his novels. Writers have often alluded to mythology, religious stories, or other works of literature from the past: these allusions often add great prestige and power to the text.

ambiguity: purposefully doubtful, uncertain or double meanings. Often writers deliberately want to suggest or imply more than one meaning in a phrase or word (see also **irony**). Ambiguity in poetry often sets out to mystify rather than clarify, so that the readers must work to make their own judgements about possible meanings. Ambiguity does not just relate to meanings — texts can have ambiguous moods and tones.

analogy: a comparison which does not use imagery. Writers often describe a situation or event which is comparable to another one; an analogy is stronger than a similarity — it will be more complex, with a number of links.

antithesis: an arrangement of words or phrases in poetry designed to stress contrasts or opposites, brought out by the positioning of the words or phrases:

> 'Fairest Cordelia, that art most rich, being poor,
> Most choice, forsaken, and most loved, despised.'
> — Shakespeare's *King Lear*, Act 1, scene 1

assonance: a combination of vowel sounds, commonly used in poetry, in order to add to the meaning:

> 'The morning-dream that hover'd o'er her head'
> — *The Rape of the Lock*, by Alexander Pope

ballad: a poem that tells a story. Ballads often rhyme, and are frequently associated with traditional stories, sometimes based on legend, often derived from old folk tales with romantic, supernatural or other atmospheric settings.

bathos: an anti-climax — a deliberate attempt by the writer to reduce an important or dramatic moment to a lesser or lower tone.

blank verse: poetry which is unrhymed. In modern times, the forms available to writers have become so open and varied that there can even be an abandonment of punctuation — the structure can be very loose indeed. Blank verse is sometimes termed **free verse**.

burlesque: farce — an attempt, often through caricature or absurd comic technique, to make a subject appear ridiculous.

cadence: the deliberate modulation of the sounds of words, usually arranged by the rhythmic form.

caesura: a break in a line of poetry. Quite often this involves a dramatic break in the meaning of a phrase.

caricature: the establishment of larger-than-life characters who appear more as stereotypes. Dickens was the great creator of caricatures — in most of his famous characters there is a representation of 'types' of well-known figures from nineteenth century life. Similarly, many of Shakespeare's minor characters are caricatures, often comic types rather than real people.

catharsis: a purging of emotions. Often great tragedy involves the flushing out of feelings or emotions, and as a result, the characters are better able to understand themselves.

characterisation: how a writer will use language to build up and reveal characters (e.g. through speech, description of appearance, actions).

chronology: a course of events which happens within a proper time sequence: novels, for example, will either occur in chronological order, beginning at the beginning and ending at the end, or will occur within disjunctions of time.

cliché: a tired, habitually overworked phrase, e.g. 'the clouds looked like cotton wool . . .'.

climax: the text leading up to an event, phrase, mood or feeling of great importance, in prose or poetry.

colloquialisms: words or phrases which are informal, familiar, part of everyday speech.

connotation: a word which carries with it a suggested or implied meaning. Names of animals (pig, fish, snake, etc.) often hold connotations — that is, the words have come to hold associations for us other than just types of animal.

dialogue: the use of conversation in literature — an important way to help create, and describe, characters.

diction: the choice of words to give a particular slant to meanings. Think of, for example, the differences suggested between *storm* and *tempest*, or *pupil* and *student*.

elegy: a poem written in someone's memory. The most famous elegy is by the poet Thomas Gray who wrote about the poor buried in a country churchyard: Gray's *Elegy in a Country Churchyard*.

enigma: literature which is deliberately puzzling, secretive, obscure or unusual.

enjambement: continuation of the sense of a poem from one line to the next.

epistle: a letter within a piece of literature.

eulogy: a form of literature written or spoken in great praise of a person, place or event. In Shakespeare, Macbeth is spoken of very highly at the start of the play, and there is a eulogy spoken by Brutus about Julius Caesar after the emperor's death.

euphemism: the use of a mild word or phrase to suggest something which is in reality more sinister or dramatic: Horatio says to Hamlet: 'So Guildenstern and Rozencrantz go to't,' — meaning that they have been put to their deaths!

evocation (evoke/evocative): the capacity of a writer to bring to life certain memories, feelings or associations — sometimes to call up a certain mood or atmosphere, or a sense of place.

fable: a work of literature founded on myth or legend, usually carrying powerful meanings and messages.

farce: the use of ridiculous characters in absurd settings and situations.

figurative language: non-literal use of language, often in the form of imagery, but sometimes as figures of speech (e.g. in sayings or proverbs).

form: the type, or structure, of a work of literature. Poems appear in the form of ballads, elegies, sonnets, odes, free verse, etc. It can be more difficult to describe the form of a prose extract, as there is less difference between one form of novel writing and another. (Some examples are: realistic, Gothic, narrative, stream of consciousness, etc.)

genre: a type or collection of writing, e.g. realistic novel, romantic, Gothic, fable, ballad, satire. The key point is that to belong to a genre, a work will contain certain distinguishing features marking it out as a particular type of writing.

Gothic: a form of literature, popular in the eighteenth-nineteenth centuries, which was eerie and forbidding in tone, often verging on the horrific or supernatural.

hero/heroine: the principal character in a novel or play, usually expected to be a decent sort of character, one who can be admired or held in high esteem.

heroic couplet: a closed, self-contained rhyming couplet of **iambic pentameters**, often very witty in tone and meaning, particularly popular in the mock-classical poetry of Johnson, Dryden and Pope in the seventeenth and early eighteenth centuries.

hyperbole: exaggeration — to coin a phrase, this is when writers 'go over the top' with their use of language, suggesting that something is the strongest, the best, the greatest, which of course distorts the truth. Another example from *The Rape of the Lock*:

'Belinda smiled, and all the world was gay'

iambic pentameter: a line in poetry consisting of five 'feet' or stresses, in which the syllables will alternate — one will be stressed, the next unstressed, as in this line from Gray's *Elegy*:

'The <u>cur</u>few <u>tolls</u> the <u>knell</u> of <u>part</u>ing <u>day</u>'

idiom: a phrase or expression in current use — similar to colloquialisms, these will be familiar, conversational, or even figurative.

imagery: a non-literal contrast. There are three common types of images: similes, metaphor and personification. These examples are taken from *The Rape of the Lock*:

(a) **similes:**

'her eyes
like the sun, shine on all alike'

(a simile makes a comparison by stating that one thing is like another).

(b) **metaphors:** in another part of the poem, the writer refers to a pair of scissors:

'The little engine on his finger's ends . . .'

(a metaphor allows the object to become the item with which it is being compared. In this case, the scissors become the little engine, and there is no need for the writer to state that they 'are like' the engine — in this way a metaphor is a more direct comparison).

(c) **personification:** this involves turning an object — either inanimate or natural — into a human or animal form, with human or animal actions and feelings. Pope is here writing about the river Thames:

'Thames with pride surveys his rising towers'

(It is essential to understand what is meant by non-literal language: eyes cannot literally be the sun; a pair of scissors cannot literally be an engine; a river cannot literally survey towers with pride!)

intrigue: the plot of a work of literature, especially when there are mysterious circumstances surrounding it, with matters to be resolved.

irony: saying, or writing, one thing, and meaning another. Think of it as a form of sarcasm, where sometimes people are 'put down' — for example, we might say 'well done' to somebody who trips over some steps! Irony in literature is much the same, and is quite often intended to make fun of characters, reveal their weaknesses, or to mock them. To find ironic language, therefore, look for hidden or double meanings.

lyric/lyrical: poetry which has the qualities of song. The words of songs are actually called lyrics, and a lot of poetry would originally have been written to be put to music. What we mean by 'lyrical writing' is that the subject and mood of the piece has a musical air to it, perhaps evoking scenes of great beauty or charm.

macabre: literature describing subjects of gruesome horror.

melancholy/melancholic: lowness or terrible depression of spirits in a character or mood.

melodrama/melodramatic: writing made particularly popular in Victorian England, characterised by the use of exaggerated characters who were either 'good' or 'bad'. It often involves exciting incidents in uncomplicated plots — a world of heroes and villains, goodies and baddies, clearly designed for popular entertainment.

Metaphysical Poetry: a term used to describe the work of a group of poets writing in the early seventeenth century, e.g. John Donne and Andrew Marvell. Their work is characterised by the development of complicated and novel images which take the reader through patterns of strained thought in order to understand striking ideas, often about love, religion, death or philosophy. Another word for these strained patterns of thought is **conceits**.

metre: the poetic rhythm which is arranged by the number of syllables in a line. Another way of thinking of the metre is as the **beat** of the poem.

mood: often used nowadays to mean tone or atmosphere. You may be asked to describe the mood of some writing, so is it sad, tragic, positive, optimistic, romantic? You can often see how mood has been created by analysing the use of adjectives and adverbs.

narrator: the teller of a story. We often talk of 'the narrator's voice': who is telling the story? Does the teller of the story play a part in it? Is it written in the first person, or the third person, by the omniscient narrator? All of this makes up **narrative technique** — the ways in which a story is written.

nostalgia/nostalgic: a feeling of loss or longing for the past.

ode: a lyrical poem which is, essentially, addressed to a person, or to an object being personified. Such verses often involve a sustained meditation about that person or object.

onomatopoeia: a word used to suggest its meaning by its sound — such as 'crash' or 'scream'. Clearly, in poetry, the effect will be less obvious, as in this example from *The Rape of the Lock*:

> 'Now lap-dogs give themselves the rousing shake'

oxymoron: a figure of speech joining together words of opposite meaning. This is another example from *The Rape of the Lock*:

> 'This day, black Omens threat the brightest Fair'

paradox: a self-contradictory statement of opposites, which nevertheless contains an element of truth.

parody: writing meant to mock another style — often to hold that style, or its writer, up to ridicule.

pathetic fallacy: the crediting of nature with human feelings. This is a technique similar to personification.

pathos: a feeling of great sadness or tone of pity in literature.

pentameter: a line of verse having five 'feet'. (See **iambic pentameter**.)

picaresque: a type of novel, made popular in the eighteenth century, which tells of wandering rogues who are subject to complicated, over-long plots. There are often scenes representing comic low-life: Defoe, Sterne, Smollett and Fielding were famous for this type of novel.

plot: the plan of events in a story or play — effectively, the plot is 'what happens', as opposed to the subject or themes.

poetic: a style used in prose writing which appears to have the more moving qualities of poetry. Some prose contains rhythm, atmospheric passages, and moments when there is great feeling and imagination engendered by the style.

prose: it is difficult to give a precise definition, but the best way to define prose is to think of it as writing which is not poetry. It is the writing most commonly found in stories and novels, and is characterised by the use of continuous sentences and paragraphs.

pun: a play on words, involving double meanings, sometimes using **homophones** — words that sound the same, but have different meanings and perhaps different spellings. Shakespeare frequently used this type of pun. *Julius Caesar* begins with a famous one: a citizen of Rome is asked what his job is, and he, a cobbler, jokingly replies that he is a 'mender of bad soles.'

realism: writing which shows life as it really is — frequently capturing a sense of the truth, almost like a photograph or descriptive painting. The effect is often created by mention of down-to-earth objects, recognisable features, or dialogue which can almost be heard, as if spoken aloud.

refrain: a recurring phrase or line, like a chorus, often found at the end of a verse — a technique often used in ballads and elsewhere.

rhetoric: nowadays we tend to use this term to mean persuasive, often elegant, language, found in speeches and argument. It can also mean a way of criticising a speaker when, for example, it can imply that he or she has used words powerfully and convincingly, but without much substance in the argument. In the past, however, rhetoric more accurately meant 'the art of speech-making'.

rhyme: words placed in a relationship in poetry, frequently at the ends of lines, due to their sounding the same.

> 'Behold, four kings in majesty revered,
> With hoary whiskers and a forky beard'
>
> *— The Rape of the Lock*

rhythm: the metre, or the beat of lines in poetry.

satire: mockery in literature, intended to poke fun at characters, in order to expose their weaknesses, their foolishness, or their immorality.

sibilance: the repeated use of 's' sounds in lines of poetry, giving the words added depth of meaning (see the example for **alliteration**).

soliloquy: a speech in a play spoken by one character to the audience only — really a character thinking aloud — a technique used a great deal by Shakespeare.

sonnet: a poem of fourteen lines of **iambic pentameters**, often about subjects of great importance such as love, death, nature, religion or the meaning of life. Elizabethan sonnets consisted of one verse, with the regular rhyming pattern *ababcdcdefefgg*; later sonnets, based on an Italian method, are often a group of eight lines (octave) in one verse, followed by a verse of six lines (sestet).

stanza: literally, a section or division of a poem, e.g. verse, couplet, sestet.

stream of consciousness: a technique of writing, more likely to be prose than poetry, in which the writer is presenting thoughts as they occur. This technique was made famous by the twentieth century writer Virginia Woolf, who wrote whole sections of her novels as if they were simply an expression of the thoughts and sensations inside the head of her characters.

stress: the way in which prose (or, more especially, poetry) allows for the emphasis of certain syllables in pronunciation.

style: that part of literature which is to do with the expression (as opposed to the content, ideas, themes or subject matter). Style is always associated with *how* literature is written rather than *what* it is about.

symbol: the use of one thing to represent or suggest something else, in literature. (We talk about objects or events being symbolic of a mood, feeling or idea, even if at first glance they do not appear related.)

theme: a key idea in a poem, play or novel (e.g. power in *Macbeth*; conscience in *Henry V*).

tone: the overall mood or feeling of writing: for example, the tone could be humorous, tragic, persuasive, mocking, or serious.

voice: a common term used to mean 'the writer's sense of presence in a piece of writing'.

REVISION OF RUBRIC INSTRUCTIONS

The activities outlined in this book have attracted a wide variety of instructions. The term 'critical appraisal' is the latest jargon for an activity which has, over the years, variously been called 'practical criticism', 'comprehension' and 'critical appreciation'.

From 1996 onwards, students are in the fortunate position (compared to their predecessors) of standing a chance of being given more explicit instructions. In the past, most rubrics stated simply: 'write an appreciation of the following text(s)', without any reference to particular points of focus. As you will see from the sections of examples and the practice material, the majority of texts nowadays are given a task which directs your attention to a specific point of focus rather than leaving you in the dark, wondering where you ought to begin. There are some questions, however, which remain very open to your interpretation.

Before you go into your exam, it might be helpful to think about the different kinds of instruction that you could be given in any task, and to revise their requirements. The most common instructions are as follows:

account for (explain): show how a feature of the text works — explain how the language brings out key ideas under scrutiny.

analyse: go into the points in detail, with reference to ideas, meanings and themes, as well as how the language works to establish the ideas.

bring out: reveal, through an analysis of ideas, themes, characterisation, etc. and show how the language contributes to those ideas.

comment on: do not be fooled by this instruction — it sounds rather tame, but it really means 'discuss' or 'analyse'.

discuss: go into all aspects — treat the work as widely as you can, whilst, of course, remaining relevant.

evaluate: make a judgement.

examine: consider all sides, maybe looking for an effect or result of a particular technique.

explore: range over a number of possible meanings and interpretations.

illustrate: bring out, with very close reference to the text.

interpret: offer ideas and meanings which arise out of the arrangement of the text.

show how: point to features in the language that contribute to the meanings and interpretations you are discussing.

state: provide arguments which are fully supported with close textual reference.

trace: again, this sounds weaker than it is — it means follow through a line of argument, pursuing it in detail with close reference.

write about: this simply means 'go into full detail'. It does depend upon you knowing the criteria by which you are marked in exams.

2 *Poetry*

In the appreciations you write about poetry, you will particularly need to:

- recognise that subject matter, themes and meanings are often interdependent;
- show understanding of tone, atmosphere and mood;
- analyse poetic techniques and relate them to meanings;
- be aware that good poetry often hints at feelings and meanings rather than stating them explicitly;
- show an understanding that there are frequently connections between ideas and images in poems;
- be sensitive to the meanings that lie beneath the surface;
- be able to draw attention to language that is moving, attractive, lyrical and beautiful;
- be able to comment on style and form as well as on content and meaning;
- show awareness of the value of imagery and symbolism.

A   A COMPARISON OF TWO POEMS

Write a critical appreciation of the following: an extract from Shakespeare's *Measure for Measure* (1604): 'Aye, but to die, and go we know not where' and *Exposure* (1917) by Wilfred Owen. Show how the writers bring out ideas and meanings connected with the subject of contemplation of death.

POEM   *(a)*   *Aye, But to Die, and Go we Know not Where*

Aye, but to die, and go we know not where;
To lie in cold obstruction and to rot;
This sensible warm motion to become
A kneaded clod; and the delighted spirit
To bathe in fiery floods, or to reside
In thrilling regions of thick-ribbed ice;
To be imprison'd in the viewless winds,
And blown with restless violence round about
The pendant world; or to be worse than worst
Of those that lawless and incertain thoughts
Imagine howling: 'tis too horrible!
The weariest and most loathed worldly life
That age, ache, penury and imprisonment
Can lay on nature is a paradise
To what we fear of death.

                                                   WILLIAM SHAKESPEARE

POEM   *(b)*   *Exposure*

Our brains ache, in the merciless iced east winds that knive us . . .
Wearied we keep awake because the night is silent . . .
Low, drooping flares confuse our memory of the salient . . .
Worried by silence, sentries whisper, curious, nervous,
          But nothing happens.

Watching, we hear the mad gusts tugging on the wire,
Like twitching agonies of men among its brambles.
Northward, incessantly, the flickering gunnery rumbles,
Far off, like a dull rumour of some other war.
        What are we doing here?

The poignant misery of dawn begins to grow . . .
We only know war lasts, rain soaks, and clouds sag stormy.
Dawn massing in the east her melancholy army
Attacks once more in ranks on shivering ranks of gray,
        But nothing happens.

Sudden successive flights of bullets streak the silence.
Less deadly than the air that shudders black with snow,
With sidelong flowing flakes that flock, pause, and renew,
We watch them wandering up and down the wind's nonchalance,
        But nothing happens.

Pale flakes with fingering stealth come feeling for our faces
We cringe in holes, back on forgotten dreams, and stare, snow-dazed,
Deep into grassier ditches. So we drowse, sun-dozed,
Littered with blossoms trickling where the blackbird fusses.
        Is it that we are dying?

Slowly our ghosts drag home: glimpsing the sunk fires, glozed
With crusted dark-red jewels; crickets jingle there;
For hours the innocent mice rejoice: the house is theirs;
Shutters and doors, all closed: on us the doors are closed, —
        We turn our back to dying.

Since we believe not otherwise can kind fires burn;
Nor ever suns smile true on child, or field, or fruit.
For God's invincible spring our love is made afraid;
Therefore, not loath, we lie out here; therefore were born,
        For love of God seems dying.

Tonight, His frost will fasten on this mud and us,
Shrivelling many hands, puckering many foreheads crisp.
The burying-party, picks and shovels in their shaking grasp,
Pause over half-known faces. All their eyes are ice,
        But nothing happens.

                              WILFRED OWEN

As you are not asked to state a preference, you should spend your time dealing equally with both texts. Because you are asked to focus on ideas and meanings, our advice would be to try to deal with both texts throughout the body of your essay. Your work may appear immature if you deal with the texts separately, particularly if this means that you are unable to make connections between the ideas.

ANSWER

The writers convey the fear and uncertainty in the contemplation of death. The moods of the poems, created by contrasting styles, contribute to the cold and fearful atmospheres in both poems.

In *Exposure*, the malevolence of the weather is intensified through Owen's use of similes and personification. The wind and the snow are especially threatening:

> 'the merciless iced east winds that knive us' and:

> 'Less deadly than the air that shudders black with snow'

The violence in these phrases immediately establishes a cold, murderous atmosphere. The snow is personified as a ghostly presence which is more frightening than the sound of bullets in the air, and which also has a connection with the idea of death coming to seek them out:

> 'Pale flakes with fingering stealth come feeling for our faces'

The alliteration in this line emphasises the omnipresence of the snowflakes and the fear they create. The deathly mood of the poem is reinforced by Owen's personification of the elements.

This mood is related throughout the poem to the situation: it is a poem about the way that men await the inevitability of death, and therefore in the discomfort of their situation: 'war lasts, rain soaks, and clouds sag stormy', this sense of fear and impending death becomes even stronger and easy to imagine. This sense of realism is portrayed throughout the poem, so that these are real soldiers having to prepare for death, already in a state of physical hardship. In the first verse, they are tormented by the silence, which has an eerie chill to it and also foretells of the death to come. The broken line: 'Worried by silence, sentries whisper, curious, nervous,' adds to this state of torment, especially as the agony is prolonged: 'But nothing happens'.

In the second verse the men seem to live outside their own experience of events:

> '. . . the flickering gunnery rumbles,
> Far off, like a dull rumour of some other war.'

This produces the idea that they are almost looking at their own mortality, which must be very uncomfortable.

As the situation worsens, mainly symbolically through the chill breath of the weather, so the soldiers become confused and enter a state of confusion in their consciousness. The refrain of 'But nothing happens' prolongs the quiet wait and tension, whilst minds begin to wander as 'So we drowse . . .'. Their ghosts 'drag home', to memories of familiar surroundings at home, and then they seem to accept the future of death with a strong religious theme as they believe they must give themselves up to the love of God for their likely impending deaths. This, in any event, is really a situation with no alternative. On the one hand they must submit themselves to their God, but there is also a mood of bitterness in God's withdrawal of love, as death is imminent:

> 'Therefore, not loath, we lie out here; therefore were born,
> For love of God seems dying.'

Death, as a form of action, and a sort of physical activity, is vividly represented in the realism of the final verse, when *God* is personified, and there is then oblivion in the final repetition of the line 'But nothing happens' which, in contrast to the earlier meaning, when the attack would 'not happen', now signifies oblivion.

These ideas are more of a contemplation of the events leading up to death. They are brought about by a situation, in the war, which must have been familiar to thousands, if not millions, of soldiers, and in that sense is full of realism. The moods and actions of the poem are corroborated through careful diction, and the ideas enhanced through the sounds of the words chosen by the poet. Owen conveys the harshness through the use of short, harsh words which employ the technique of onomatopoeia, such as 'ache', 'mad', 'streak', 'flock'. He also conveys a sense of life ebbing away in verbs such as 'tugging', 'twitching', 'flickering' and 'puckering'. All of these words bring over the bitterness and gall of the final hours on the battlefield.

Examiner's comment

> A very competent discussion of *Exposure*, with a willingness to tackle the realism of the situation in the poem, along with some of the moods and contrasts created by it. The ambiguity of the religious theme is also approached with a willingness to analyse the double meanings. We recognise that in the short time available, any discussion of the poem will be limited as there is a great deal in it, and this candidate has been quite selective. So far, there has been reference to imagery: the examiner will be looking out to see to what extent this candidate might be able to deal with the symbolism elsewhere in the remainder of the answer.

Shakespeare's verse from *Measure for Measure* takes a very different view of the subject. The nightmarish thoughts of the persona are clearly defined as mere thoughts of what is to come after death. The philosophical element of this poem establishes the fact that they are purely thoughts, although they do present, as Owen does, a disturbing view of death.

For Shakespeare, the uncertainty comes not through thoughts of when death will happen — unlike Owen's poem, it is not a poem about the last moments of life, but transfers to the first moments of death, and so immediately the terror of this uncertainty is brought out in the words: 'and go we know not where'. All in all, Shakespeare might be describing a vision of hell in this scene, with an impression that, after death, we will suffer the torments of enduring the elements of earth, air and water, and all of these agonies will be experienced in an awful and cruel way:

> 'To bathe in fiery floods'; and

> 'To be imprison'd in the viewless winds'.

This constant reminder of the hell-like conditions envisaged in death are then part of an argument that Shakespeare accentuates in his poem, which is that the worst things in life are better than this awful vision. The worst features of life are:

> '. . . a paradise
> To what we fear of death.'

As in Owen's poem, the cold harsh words used by Shakespeare contribute to the insensitive, cold attitude of nature towards death, words such as: 'cold', 'rot', 'clod' and 'thick'. As well as this cold terror, Shakespeare also conjures up an impression of the dead being restless and imprisoned in the hell they discover. The world of this hell is sometimes created in dramatic tones, e.g. with the alliteration in: 'To bathe in fiery floods', and with the strong assonance in the line: 'And blown with restless violence round about.' This is a line which we can almost imagine having the corresponding movement in it, it is so strong.

Examiner's comment

Competence and confidence with technical details of poetic technique.

The ideas and meanings surrounding the issue of contemplation of death are presented through the structures of the verses. Owen presents his thoughts in a directly poetic manner, whereas Shakespeare's, as part of a play, are part of a speech or soliloquy. Shakespeare's language is a build up of ideas, these ideas flow from one to the other, leading to a conclusion which is a comparison with life. Owen's poem to some extent tells a story. It is a chronological account of life on a battlefield. The pauses at end-stopped lines in *Exposure* allow time for sympathy and emphasise the silence experienced by the expectant and tense soldiers, when all the time, in the refrain, 'nothing happens.' There are also important contrasts in *Exposure*, as part of the poem's structure, for example in their dreams they visualise the 'blossoms trickling where the blackbird fusses', but this also stresses the immediate situation, as the blossom could be the frost on the battlefield.

In both poems the combination of poetic devices and diction enhance the vivid images which contain meanings and ideas. Shakespeare's are about a vision of life after death, but in a way this hellish vision also shows why human beings fear death so much. Owen's are about the fear of dying, which to the soldiers in their game of waiting, especially in such severe weather conditions, is a very real fear.

Examiner's comment

Excellent, if not always stylish in expression. This candidate moves from discussion of the content, meanings and ideas, through to a worthy consideration of technique, and with good points of reference. It is also encouraging to find an answer where form and structure figure in the analysis.

B DIFFERENT APPROACHES IN POETRY

The two poems, *Snakecharmer*, by Sylvia Plath and *In the Snake Park*, by William Plomer, seek, in different ways, to invite us into the world of the snake. Both are mid-twentieth century poems. Comment on the different approaches and techniques which the poets use, and on their effectiveness.

POEM

(a)   *Snakecharmer*

As the gods began one world, and man another,
So the snakecharmer begins a snaky sphere
With moon-eye, mouth-pipe. He pipes. Pipes green. Pipes water.

Pipes water green until green waters waver
With reedy lengths and necks and undulatings.
And as his notes twine green, the green river

Shapes its images around his songs.
He pipes a place to stand on, but no rocks,
No floor: a wave of flickering grass tongues

Supports his foot. He pipes a world of snakes,
Of sways and coilings, from the snake-rooted bottom
Of his mind. And now nothing but snakes

Is visible. The snake-scales have become
Leaf, become eyelid; snake-bodies, bough, breast
Of tree and human. And he within this snakedom

Rules the writhings which make manifest
His snakehood and his might with pliant tunes
From his thin pipe. Out of his green nest

As out of Eden's navel twist the lines
Of snaky generations: let there be snakes!
And snakes there were, are, will be — till yawns

Consume the piper and he tires of music
And pipes the world back to the simple fabric
Of snake-warp, snake-weft. Pipes the cloth of snakes

To a melting of green waters, till no snake
Shows its head, and those green waters back to
Water, to green, to nothing like a snake.
Puts up his pipe, and lids his moony eye.

SYLVIA PLATH

(b)   *In the Snake Park*

POEM

A white-hot midday in the Snake Park.
Lethargy lay here and there in coils,
And here and there a neat obsidian head
Lay dreaming on a plaited yellow pillow of its own
Loops like a pretzel or a true-love-knot.

A giant Python seemed a heap of tyres;
Two Nielsen's Vipers looked for a way out,
Sick of their cage and one another's curves;
And the long Ringsnake brought from Lembuland
Poured slowly through an opening like smoke.

Leaning intently forward a young girl
Discerned in stagnant water on a rock
A dark brown shoestring or discarded whiplash,
Then read the label to find out the name,
Then stared again: it moved. She screamed.

Old Poet Vander leant with us that day
On the low wall around the rocky space
Where amid the broken quartz that cast no shade
Snakes twitched or slithered, or appeared to sleep,
Or lay invisible in the singing glare.

The sun throbbed like a fever as he spoke:
'Look carefully at this shrub with glossy leaves.'
Leaves bright as brass. 'That leaf on top
Just there, do you see that it has eyes?
That's a Green Mamba, and it's watching you.

'A man I once knew did survive the bite,
Saved by a doctor running with a knife,
Serum and all. He was never the same again.
Vomiting blackness, agonising, passing blood,
Part paralysed, near gone, he felt

'(He told me later) he would burst apart;
But the worst agony was in his mind —
Unbearable nightmare, worse than total grief
Or final loss of hope, impossibly magnified
To a blind person of panic and extreme distress.'

'Why should that little head have power
To inject all horror for no reason at all?'
'Ask me another — and beware of snakes.'
The sun was like a burning-glass. Face down
The girl who screamed had fallen in a faint.

WILLIAM PLOMER

Examiner's tip

The examiner is here inviting you to explore each poem, but it is important to note that there is no suggestion that one poem is more effective than the other and you are not expected to state a preference.

Perhaps the fascination of the first poet is with the undulating movement of the snake: comparison with reeds moving in water, and many other linguistic tricks, are used to show and explore that movement — the use of alliteration is obvious, but you must comment on the ways that individual words work to intertwine with others.

There is a character in the first poem, the snake charmer, but he is almost unreal and is there only as creator of the movement and the mystery. The second poet is more concerned with human attitudes and relationships. There is a variety of images, the beautiful and the harsh. The examiner would be interested to see what you make of the somnolent beauty of the first verse, the clumsiness ('heap of tyres') of the second, through to the violence and almost objectionable nature of the final verse, especially the final line. What sorts of attitudes towards the snakes are invited by the poets? Are they contrasting?

You really ought to comment on the intention of each poet in using their particular approach, and because these are poems which have been skilfully crafted, with many techniques, you should comment on technique in some detail, perhaps drawing attention to the contrasting forms, the sound patterns, imagery, alliteration, personification, and even the characterisation.

ANSWER

Letts Q&A

The two poems seek to demonstrate, in different ways, various aspects of the snakes' natures, and both poems also present a view of the relationship that human beings have with such curious creatures.

In the first stanza of *Snakecharmer*, we are really looking at the world through the eyes of a snake, and then for most of the poem the world and the varied movements of the snake are expressed more through the symbols in the snake charmer's musical activity than through any description of snakes. The pipe that the snake charmer plays reminds the snake of the sound of the reeds rustling in the wild. The colour green also becomes important, reminding the snake of the colour of the reeds and vegetation in its natural surroundings.

The intentions of the poem begin to merge so that we are partly in the world of the snake, partly watching the work of the snake charmer, and, as well as this, we are given a wider view of the world of nature:

> 'Pipes water green until green waters waver
> With reedy lengths and necks and undulatings.'

Alliteration is used to great effect in these lines when describing the water and the snake's movements. There is a dual purpose to this pattern of sounds: firstly the sounds of the words remind the reader of the sounds of the snake, and secondly, the words weave together, which is reminiscent of the snake weaving through the weeds. In the third and fourth stanzas the imagery used to describe the form of the snake is also very strong:

> 'Shapes its images around his songs'

This line presents a view of the snake swaying and contorting under the exotic influence of the snake charmer's music. This is continued with the lines in the fourth stanza, which again concentrate on the movement of the snake and present a view of the work of the snake charmer:

> '. . . He pipes a world of snakes,
> Of sways and coilings'

What this is showing is that there are two main ways in which the poem is developing, a view of the movements and life of the snake and the world of snakes in the imagination of the charmer.

The fifth stanza is devoted to the snake's deceptive appearance, and how well camouflaged the snake is in the tree:

> '. . . The snake-scales have become
> Leaf, become eyelid'

There is further double-meaning here, from the play on the word 'scales', which means obviously the scales on the snake's skin, but could also bring to mind the music of the charmer.

Further on in the poem, the writer applies human terms in relation to the snake — 'snakedom' and 'snakehood'. There is also a Biblical reference which draws a similarity between the snake and mankind: 'Out of Eden's navel', the place where Adam and Eve were expelled after being tempted by the serpent and from which the generations of man and snake have both evolved. The phrase: 'let there be snakes!' reminds us of God's proclamation, 'Let there be light!' at the earth's creation. This is another point in the poem where the connections between the ideas about the snake and about man's life are drawn together. As the piper tires of playing his pipe, the world of snakes leaves his imagination, and once again, the picture that the piper has woven disintegrates, and finally, he lays his pipe to rest and sleeps. In this ending of the poem there is another merging together of strains which have been evident earlier. The images of weaving and melting of green waters are expressed again to show the collapse of this magical moment in life. It is not just the snake which returns to its original position, but also the world, losing its momentary excitement. This is a very good example of how the poet can take a subject, in this case the snake, and make available extra meanings which are woven into the structure of the poem.

The structure is fairly uniform, with stanzas one to eight composed of three lines each, and the final stanza of four lines. To me this somehow recreates the tune and measured movement of the charmer and snake, although there are also important breaks in the punctuation which can also come to mean the change in the tune and the direction of the snake's undulating movements.

Examiner's comment

The analysis of this poem has been detailed. It is a complex poem, with many connotations rather than explicit meanings, and so it was sensible of the candidate to deal with the poems separately, leaving the second poem for later consideration. Perhaps, if time permitted, the imagery and the religious references could have been more fully explored, but the examiner recognises that this has been a fairly full and progressive analysis and one which certainly brings out some of the duality of meaning in the poem. The candidate has not avoided this difficulty of dealing with double meanings (is the poem about the snake, about the actions of the charmer, about the world of nature or about human life?) which might have characterised the work of a weaker candidate.

The second poem, *In the Snake Park*, opens with an entirely different atmosphere created, written in a style similar to that of a story. The poet describes the snakes lying in the midday sun as 'lethargy'. The description is exact and detailed. The poet presents a view to the reader of the snakes' huge body mass and small neat black heads. This precision and intricacy of description is further developed in the similes of 'a pretzel or a true-love-knot'. This conjures a complicated visual picture of looping bodies hanging and threading, and sets a tone of realism. It could also be said to start the tone of dislike and discomfort which is something felt later, especially by the girl. This comes out, for example, because the image of the pretzel is an ugly one, knotted and twisted.

The poet continues in a descriptive manner, and uses other similes to emphasise the snakes' appearance, comparing the python in a rather odd way to a 'heap of tyres'. This is an uncomfortable image and puts the snake over in an ugly, disgusting manner, so we are prepared for the reactions of the people to the snakes later in the poem.

They are seeking a way out of their cage, like their tongues seeking a way out of their 'neat obsidian heads'. This is perhaps threatening. Compared to the first poem, there is a build up in this poem of a narrative expressing fear and repulsiveness, whereas in *Snakecharmer* the delight of the snake's movements was always at the forefront of the poet's mind. In the second poem, the movements of the snakes are described like smoke pouring through an opening, which is highly suggestive of the snakes' smooth liquidity.

Stanzas three and four are mainly narrative, describing the surprise of the girl who realised that it wasn't a discarded shoestring or whiplash she was looking at, but a snake. The account of the throbbing heat reminds us of the natural habitat of the snake, and also prepares us for the terrible story about the venom of the Green Mamba. As this story is introduced in stanza six, the whole tone of the poem is reversed, introducing a new rhythm, one of fear and anxiety in the actions. The deceptive lethargy described at first has given way to the gruesome account of someone who is bitten by a poisonous snake, and as a result is suffering unbearable mental torture. It is at this point in the poem that I become convinced that there is no sympathy for the world of the snake from this poet: unlike the first poet, here the snake is seen as a devious, deceptive and life-threatening beast, rather than a thing of beauty. Whereas *Snakecharmer* expressed the traditional fascination with the sensual movement of the snake, this poem raises another traditional view which is often the idea of deceptive violence in the snake. The poet even makes this point as a direct question:

> 'Why should that little head have power
> To inject all horror for no reason at all?'

Then finally, the action of the girl fainting is a conclusion to the horror of the snakes. It is there to remind us just how dreadful they can appear, and in a way her reaction is a symbol of human attitudes to these deadly animals.

Examiner's comment

> The candidate here follows the same formula as has been used in analysing the first poem — a careful, informed progress through the poem, making points which cover both the ideas and the techniques. In doing so, points of comparison with the attitude of the first poet become apparent.

Both poets endeavour to relay to the reader different aspects of the world of the snake, in sharply contrasting situations: *Snakecharmer* in an exotic world of music and imagination, with a touch also of philosophy brought out by the evolution of snake and man. In *In the Snake Park* there is a situation of human beings looking at the snakes and reacting with a mood that stresses aspects of terror and fear. The effectiveness of these different aspects lies in the poets' use of such techniques as imagery and alliteration.

Examiner's comment

> The final sentence adds very little, although in the first part of this conclusion there is an effort made to summarise the important differences in the poets' attitudes.
> The essay has analysed the poems in considerable detail, points of comparison have been made successfully, and some of the poetic techniques are revealed. There is certainly an understanding of style and purpose. Finally, the candidate's own writing is quite well organised. There has been no problem with the way that she worked through each poem individually, mainly because she was able to draw out points of comparison as the discussion of the second poem progressed.

C COMPARING TWO POEMS ON SIMILAR SUBJECTS

Compare the two poems that follow: *After Apple-picking*, by Robert Frost (1916), and *Apples*, by Laurie Lee (1964).

(a)   *After Apple-picking*

POEM

> My long two-pointed ladder's sticking through a tree
> Toward heaven still,
> And there's a barrel that I didn't fill
> Beside it, and there may be two or three
> Apples I didn't pick upon some bough.
> But I am done with apple-picking now.
> Essence of winter sleep is on the night,
> The scent of apples: I am drowsing off.
> I cannot rub the strangeness from my sight
> I got from looking through a pane of glass
> I skimmed this morning from the drinking trough
> And held against the world of hoary grass.

It melted, and I let it fall and break.
But I was well
Upon my way to sleep before it fell,
And I could tell
What form my dreaming was about to take.
Magnified apples appear and disappear,
Stem end and blossom end,
And every fleck of russet showing clear.
My instep arch not only keeps the ache,
It keeps the pressure of a ladder-round.
I feel the ladder sway as the boughs bend.
And I keep hearing from the cellar bin
The rumbling sound
Of load on load of apples coming in.
For I have had too much
Of apple-picking: I am overtired.
Of the great harvest I myself desired.
There were ten thousand thousand fruit to touch,
Cherish in hand, lift down, and not let fall.
For all
That struck the earth,
No matter if not bruised or spiked with stubble,
Went sure to the cider-apple heap
As of no worth.
One can see what will trouble
This sleep of mine, whatever sleep it is.
Were he not gone,
The woodchuck could say whether it's like his
Long sleep, as I describe its coming on,
Or just some human sleep.

ROBERT FROST

POEM *(b)*   *Apples*

Behold the apples' rounded worlds:
juice-green of July rain,
the black polestar of flowers, the rind
mapped with its crimson stain.

The russet, crab and cottage red
burn to the sun's hot brass,
then drop like sweat from every branch
and bubble in the grass.

They lie as wanton as they fall,
and where they fall and break,
the stallion clamps his crunching jaws,
the starling stabs his beak.

In each plump gourd the cidery bite
of boys' teeth tears the skin;
the waltzing wasp consumes his share,
the bent worm enters in.

I, with as easy hunger, take
entire my season's dole;
welcome the ripe, the sweet, the sour,
the hollow and the whole.

LAURIE LEE

Examiner's tip

This question is more bland than any presented so far — the candidate is left to decide what best to focus on. This is because there are similarities in subject matter, and contrasting themes in the poems, and you would therefore be expected to make a direct comparison.

The most important thing to do here is plan! It is no good just embarking on your answer and writing indiscriminately on the poems, without having made some decisions about your areas of comparative focus. There are, in fact, many points that could be made, but the important task is to identify and discuss some that are relevant. It could be that you will compare the narrative structure of Frost's poem with the descriptive approach of Lee; this might involve showing how Frost's style is more directly a stream of his consciousness, compared to the crafted poetic style used by Laurie Lee, in whose poem there is a lot more imagery. You might consider how the world of nature is used in both poems, in a way that is broader than simply focusing on the main subject of apples.

Finally, an examiner will be looking out to see how well you have handled the attitudes of the writers to their subjects: in *After Apple-picking*, what is the writer experiencing in relation to the ending of a season, and are there themes on a broader canvas about life generally being expressed here? Similarly, in *Apples*, what are the wider meanings of the last verse?

ANSWER

A sense of the importance of seasons is clear in both poems, but is particularly relevant to Frost's *After Apple-picking*. The apple harvesting incorporates attributes of autumn for wider symbolic effect. The cyclical birth and death of nature, the 'blossom end', can be aligned with the writer's own mortality. This is first signalled in line two, as the harvester's ladder is said to lean 'toward heaven'. The first indication that the poem will have a deeper significance is in the choice of the word 'heaven', which is later to be defined euphemistically as 'human sleep'. This is intensified during lines six and seven when the fatigue of man and nature are seen to unite:

> 'But I am done with apple-picking now.
> Essence of winter sleep is on the night,
> The scent of apples: I am drowsing off.'

Examiner's comment

A very confident opening to the essay. This is a good example of the sort of essay which has an immediate focus. The candidate is directly discussing the first poem and the examiner immediately feels confident that he will cope with the demands.

The long first line of the poem, the variation in length of other lines, and the broken punctuation, allow the poem to open in a disjointed way, as if the poet is trying to lead into the consideration and resolution of a problem about understanding his own mortality. The effect of this constant enjambement is to slow the pace and allow for the reflective conscious tone to emerge, telling us something about the state of the writer's mind.

The overall tone of the poem is in fact rather pessimistic. The title not only signals the end of the harvest, but the end of the fruitfulness of life. There are striking symbols to support this concern — a sense of lack of fulfilment in the poor harvest: 'a barrel that I didn't fill' and a feeling of hopeless lethargy associated with the apples that 'I didn't pick'.

This brooding theme of pessimism and doom in life can be compared with the celebration of the apple and sense of natural abundance that we find in *Apples*. The writer uses colour to furnish his poem with a mood of joy and delight in the apples: 'the russet, crab and cottage red' offer this mood of warmth. The poem also has a quality of succulence about it, bringing out how delicious the apples are and how much they are part of the store of nature: they 'drop like sweat' . . . the apple is a 'plump gourd'.

Whereas Frost needed a brooding narrative voice, placing himself in the poem as an authoritative narrator to express the diminishing mortality of his own mood, Lee uses a form of writing which is brighter and more of a celebration. Thus the stanzas are regular, carried along with a powerful metre and regular rhyme, almost as if to sing and shout of the succulent beauty and delicacy of the apples. In *After Apple-picking*, Frost views the events with critical intrusion and reflects on his ideas, which are a reaction to the harvest. This has three crucial moments of reflection.

Examiner's comment

We are impressed with the way that this candidate is able to integrate discussion of meaning with some of the techniques being used in the poems. There is a strong awareness of both meaning and language.

First of all, he describes the drowsiness that overcomes him from looking through a lump of ice removed from the drinking trough. There is a morning frost developing on the grass. As he surveys the late autumn scene, there is a warning to him of the winter to come, and we realise that this is symbolic, as suggested above:

> 'I cannot rub the strangeness from my sight
> I got from looking through a pane of glass'

Secondly, there is a striking theme of disappointment. The poet describes how he has hoped for a great harvest, and has dreamed of this through the 'rumbling sound/Of load on load of apples coming in'. Commenting on his own exhaustion with life — 'For I have had too much' — he then goes on to describe the disappointment in the waste of apples which:

> 'Went sure to the cider-apple heap
> As of no worth.'

Finally, there is a symbolic feeling, which could even be death, brought out in the link with the hibernation of the woodchuck.

By comparison, all of Lee's description of the apples leads to one powerful idea at the end of the poem: that is a love of the natural world, which is actually quite romantic and contented. If you look closely at the build up of this positive mood, it is not difficult to see how the apples, and nature around them, have brought it about. In the first verse there is a sensual scene, and there is an interesting use of the metaphor of the apples being 'worlds' — suggesting both their shape and the naturalness of their growth. In the second verse the colours and varieties suggest abundance and plenty, another important point about the gift of nature. Then the third verse brings in the rest of the natural world. There is a tone of temptation in the line:

> 'They lie as wanton as they fall,'

and then we see the stallion and the starling approaching the apples. I find the alliteration here very active, bringing nature strongly to life. The apples continue to be devoured in the fourth verse, and so it is hardly surprising that the writer should arrive at his philosophy of enjoying ('take entire') the gifts of nature ('season's dole') with such enthusiasm in the final verse. But, just as Frost suggests the wider mood of despair and exhaustion, so Lee accepts all parts of life, welcoming:

> '. . . the ripe, the sweet, the sour,
> the hollow and the whole.'

This makes me ask if his philosophy is to put up with a great deal in life, as suggested by the variety in nature. It is interesting how, from the two poems, we can see the themes of fruit bringing out themes of abundance and unfulfilment, the latter perhaps rather unpredictable.

Examiner's comment

Overall, a concise but very confident comparison. The issues about life which lie beyond the description of the apples or apple picking in the subject are confronted with an ease of understanding, and the answer at times is quite deep and analytical. This candidate has not necessarily been totally thorough with references, but it is clear that the poems are understood and the points of comparison are relevant. One point to emerge from this answer is that a short answer, providing it is concise and relevant, is often of merit.

D ANALYSIS OF A SINGLE POEM

Rhapsody on a Windy Night (1917) is one of T S Eliot's earlier poems. Study it carefully and then write a full appreciation of the poem.

POEM

Rhapsody on a Windy Night

> Twelve o'clock.
> Along the reaches of the street
> Held in a lunar synthesis,
> Whispering lunar incantations
> Dissolve the floors of memory
> And all its clear relations,
> Its divisions and precisions.
> Every street lamp that I pass
> Beats like a fatalistic drum,
> And through the spaces of the dark
> Midnight shakes the memory
> As a madman shakes a dead geranium.
>
> Half-past one,
> The street-lamp sputtered,
> The street-lamp muttered,
> The street-lamp said, 'Regard that woman
> Who hesitates toward you in the light of the door
> Which opens on her like a grin.
> You see the border of her dress

Is torn and stained with sand,
And you see the corner of her eye
Twists like a crooked pin.'

    The memory throws up high and dry
A crowd of twisted things;
A twisted branch upon the beach
Eaten smooth, and polished
As if the world gave up
The secret of its skeleton,
Stiff and white.
A broken spring in a factory yard,
Rust that clings to the form that the strength has left
Hard and curled and ready to snap.

    Half-past two,
The street-lamp said,
'Remark the cat which flattens itself in the gutter,
Slips out its tongue
And devours the morsel of rancid butter.'
So the hand of the child, automatic,
Slipped out and pocketed a toy that was running along the quay.
I could see nothing behind that child's eye.
I have seen eyes in the street
Trying to peer through lighted shutters,
And a crab one afternoon in a pool,
An old crab with barnacles on his back,
Gripped the end of a stick which I held him.

    Half-past three,
The lamp sputtered,
The lamp muttered in the dark.
The lamp hummed:
'Regard the moon,
La lune ne garde aucune rancune,
She winks a feeble eye,
She smiles into corners.
She smooths the hair of the grass.
The moon has lost her memory.
A washed-out smallpox cracks her face,
Her hand twists a paper rose,
That smells of dust and eau de Cologne,
She is alone
With all the old nocturnal smells
That cross and cross her brain.'
The reminiscence comes
Of sunless dry geraniums
And dust in crevices,
Smells of chestnuts in the streets,
And female smells in shuttered rooms
And cigarettes in corridors
And cocktail smells in bars.

The lamp said,
'Four o'clock,
Here is the number on the door.
Memory!
You have the key,
The little lamp spreads a ring on the stair.
Mount.
The bed is open; the tooth-brush hangs on the wall,
Put your shoes at the door, sleep, prepare for life.'

The last twist of the knife.

T S ELIOT

Examiner's tip

In writing a full appreciation of the poem, you are asked to analyse carefully, almost on a line by line basis, and then to stand back and form an impression of the whole. Your response is expected to be personal, so there is no one particular response which you are required to make.

In this tip we do not wish to encourage you along a particular route, but will simply point you to various moments which you must look at and develop. The 'lunar synthesis' calls attention to the time of day, and the street lamps are picked up in several ways as key to the atmosphere. Who is the 'madman' and is there any significance in the 'dead geranium'? Who or what is the woman in the doorway? Where are we — is the reference to the beach simply a development from the colour of her dress? It is important that you work your way through the poem asking yourself question after question. Finally consider the ending:

'. . . prepare for life.

The last twist of the knife.'

With this poem your concentration must be on content and analysis rather than on form, but don't forget that the form is not an accident. You might look on it as a series of movements which pick up points and take them forward.

ANSWER

The poem is an unusual one, so much so that a lot of its meaning seems unclear until the reader starts to visualise some of the pictures it presents and then organise these into ideas in the mind. Only then do some of the meanings start to become clear, although it is probably not possible to explain everything. This remains so because the poem is more like an abstract painting which of course does not have clear images to understand, but is always more likely to be a hotch-potch of ideas. One of the main things that the images and pictures give the reader is a mood to the poem, and this, a sort of disturbing atmosphere, is stronger in presence than a story or events, although there does appear to be some kind of situation. Towards the end of the poem this has clearly moved the main narrator of the poem into a house or room, and there is another character, a woman, involved in the scene, but it is never clear who she is or what relationship she has with the narrator.

In the next part of my essay, I am going to describe some of the moods expressed by the pictures and images. The first verse creates a mood of fatalism in the dark of night. The character is subjected to the misty loneliness of the night and as a result of this he is almost drugged into becoming something out of his own mind. The misty, moonlit night, represented by the street lamps and 'Whispering lunar incantations' takes the poet into an unreal world where everything in his normal mode of thought has changed:

'All (memory's) clear relations
Its divisions and precisions'

have been 'dissolved'. Therefore the poet has become like an alien in his own life. This could be suggesting some sort of criticism of the world in which the poet moves, and two possibilities strike me as plausible: one is that it is a very urban world, maybe in a large, anonymous city; the other is that it is a red-light district, which again is suggestive of an alienating and distressing experience for the character. It could be that the fatalism in the 'beat of the drum' is the inevitable nocturnal journey that the main character is making towards the prostitute.

It seems important that the poet follows time through the night, and as it is 'Half-past one' in the second verse, the night and its shady characters become even more distressing and sinister. The most shocking of these is symbolised in the ghastly impression to which the personified street-lamp points:

'The street-lamp said,"Regard that woman . . ." '

Her grin, the stain of sand on her dress and the way that the corner of her eye 'Twists like a crooked pin', all present an impression of somebody who can only add to the misery and despair already conjured up in the murky night.

It is difficult to guess who this woman might be, although, as already stated, one possibility is that she is actually a prostitute. However, having seen her, the memory of her then brings out other images which begin to be expressed in the third verse, and these images all contain ideas or symbols which have to be widely interpreted. The first one, the 'twisted branch upon the beach' is like human nature revealed as naked and true, but with the twist also that it is unpleasant and even rather horrific. This vision of the unpleasant side to the nature of the world is then continued with the image of the 'broken spring in a factory yard'. If this is the woman, then it is a revolting symbol, with the rust clinging to the form of the spring 'Hard and curled and ready to snap', bringing out, surely, ideas about the miserable state of human feelings. It is hard to be absolutely precise, but this symbol conjures up impressions of meanness and nastiness, perhaps also of anger and tension. My overall conclusion about these two symbols, in which the poet wants to say something frank about the woman, is that they represent the decline in human feelings rather than looking at them in a positive and loving way.

Examiner's comment

> In an analysis of this difficult poem, this candidate has, in these opening paragraphs, managed to pick her way through the difficulties with considerable skill. The examiner would be impressed by the way she has managed to interpret ideas from the series of images, especially when they have no clear explanation, and are only impressions rather than ideas. So far, the essay is also methodical, which was the mode of work suggested in the tip. It is refreshing to find this candidate willing to explore some of the wider ideas implicit in the symbols of the third verse.

In the next verse the symbols and images seem to me to become deliberately quite obscure, and the reader has to work quite hard in their own mind to be helped to picture the suggestions. The street lamps again are doing all the controlling: they are at the centre of the structure of the poem as if whoever it is, the character, or the poet, is walking aimlessly around being moved on towards a final fate by the lamps. The images of the cat and the child share one thing in common: they are both reflex actions, so maybe they are there to suggest that in this world of night and despair, no one does anything independently, but all

behaviour is reflex and mechanical. This could be said to be adding to the theme of fatalism and control which are strong in other parts of the text. Towards the end of the verse, the depression deepens — it is as if nobody can really see the world around them:

> 'I have seen eyes in the street
> Trying to peer through lighted shutters'

This brings out the disturbing idea that there is a meaning in the poem of human life being caged in, with one person not being able to relate to another. Perhaps the crab trying to 'grip the end of a stick' is like a final grasping of hope, again as if there is despair in its movements. This is surely one of the most shocking and uncomfortable images in the poem, especially as the old crab has 'barnacles on his back'.

Examiner's comment

Discussion of central ideas, the capacity to make connections between different parts of the poem, and a continuing willingness to be analytical. This candidate is also aware of how various elements relate to major themes which are being interpreted.

In the part which follows, the moon and the woman appear to have merged. In my opinion, the extended image of the moon here is far more than just that of a seductive woman, but as the prostitute, as already argued. Whatever the image the poet finally had in mind, it is once again very disturbing, and never a very pleasant situation of human contact. She (the moon or the woman) is scarred: 'A washed-out smallpox cracks her face' and she is isolated, again promoting the theme that human beings inhabit a world where they do not relate to each other any more:

> 'She is alone
> With all the old nocturnal smells
> That cross and cross her brain'

The poet makes a connection with the first verse through the symbol of the geraniums, which have come to suggest to him this barren and dry urban landscape. A strong urban landscape is further developed, painting a backdrop of life against which human beings live in despair, in an unsatisfactory mode of existence. This scene is established through:

> 'Smells of chestnuts in the streets,
> And female smells in shuttered rooms
> And cigarettes in corridors
> And cocktail smells in bars.'

Here there is a good example of the way that a poet can appeal to other senses as well as sight. The reader can sense the tawdry scenes through smell. It strikes me that all these images have in common the idea of an urban social life, but the question we are left with is whether people are really brought together or whether the truth is different? It may be that there is more of an idea that this is some kind of urban and human desert, where there is as much destruction and despair as there is love and companionship.

Examiner's comment

In the paragraph above we see a good example of personal response. Notice that it is not just a statement of what the candidate thinks, but that the personal views are argued through.

By the final verse, the night has moved on. It is four o'clock. The poet, narrator, or main character, has arrived. It is a familiar, realistic scene, but this leads into a climax which, like earlier parts of the poem, is sinister and fatalistic. There is some irony in the phrase: 'sleep, prepare for life', as life has not really been interpreted as worthwhile in other parts of the poem. Then finally, there is an interpretation that sleep is: 'The last twist of the knife', and in this way, is the life described in the poem to be seen as self-destructive?

Examiner's comment

It seems appropriate for the candidate to raise a question here. This can sometimes be acceptable style, especially if, as here, there is obscurity, irony, or ambiguity in the lines of the poem. It may not always work, so don't overuse questions as a technique of style.

In terms of the style and form of the poem, there are some important aspects which help to add to the images and mood. There is a sense of progress in the development from one separate verse to the next. This separation makes each verse into clear parts of the poem, so that the poet or narrator is taken along with fate. The other striking features are the regular rhythm, repetition and sometimes rhyme which frequently occur. At times this all gives the poem a mood, again of fate, almost as if the ideas can be seen to be part of an ancient legend, although set in a modern urban landscape. To my mind, also, the rhythms make the ideas of the poem insistent and unrelenting, as there is no escape from the truth of them, just as there is no escape from the street lamps or the night:

> 'The street-lamp sputtered,
> The street-lamp muttered,
> The street lamp said,'

Overall, the style of the poem helps to create an impression of the way that despair in this disturbing setting cannot be avoided.

Examiner's comment

We are impressed by this conclusion on style and form. It is concise, and relates well to other parts of the essay. The points about the rhythm especially are well-spotted and are another example of a sound personal response from this candidate.

All in all, a commendable attempt to deal with a difficult poem. The candidate has admitted areas of obscurity where they exist in the deliberate impressionism of the poem, whilst at the same time, working through a more than adequate personal response.

E   COMPARING REACTIONS IN POETRY

The following poems, *The Night Wind*, by Emily Brontë, and *Wind*, by Ted Hughes, are both a study of the attitudes and feelings expressed by human beings in reaction to wind. Emily Brontë wrote her poem in 1840; Ted Hughes' poem is a modern work, written in 1957.

Compare the poems. Analyse the different ways in which the poets have treated their subject matter, and consider the relations and attitudes that are shown to exist between human beings and natural elements.

Which poem strikes you as more successful in its treatment of the subject?

(a) *The Night Wind*

In summer's mellow midnight,
A cloudless moon shone through
Our open parlour window
And rosetrees wet with dew.

I sat in silent musing,
The soft wind waved my hair:
It told me Heaven was glorious,
And sleeping Earth was fair.

I needed not its breathing
To bring such thoughts to me;
But still it whispered lowly;
'How dark the woods will be!

'The thick leaves in my murmur
Are rustling like a dream,
And all their myriad voices
Instinct with spirit seem.'

I said, 'Go, gentle singer,
Thy wooing voice is kind,
But do not think its music
Has power to reach my mind.

'Play with the scented flower,
The young tree's supple bough,
And leave my human feelings
In their own course to flow.'

The wanderer would not leave me;
Its kiss grew warmer still —
'Oh come,' it sighed so sweetly,
'I'll win thee 'gainst thy will.

'Have we not been childhood friends?
Have I not loved thee long?
As long as thou hast loved the night
Whose silence wakes my song

'And when thy heart is laid at rest
Beneath the church-yard stone
I shall have time enough to mourn
And thou to be alone.'

EMILY BRONTË

(b) *Wind*

This house has been far out at sea all night,
The woods crashing through darkness, the booming hills,
Winds stampeding the fields under the window
Floundering black astride and blinding wet

Till day rose; then under an orange sky
The hills had new places, and wind wielded
Blade-light, luminous black and emerald,
Flexing like the lens of a mad eye.

At noon I scaled along the house-side as far as
The coal-house door. I dared once to look up —
Through the brunt wind that dented the balls of my eyes
The tent of the hills drummed and strained its guyrope,

The fields quivering, the skyline a grimace,
At any second to bang and vanish with a flap:
The wind flung a magpie away and a black-
Back gull bent like an iron bar slowly. The house

Rang like some fine green goblet in the note
That any second would shatter it. Now deep
In chairs, in front of the great fire, we grip
Our hearts and cannot entertain book, thought,

Or each other. We watch the fire blazing
And feel the roots of the house move, but sit on,
Seeing the window tremble to come in,
Hearing the stones cry out under the horizons.

TED HUGHES

Examiner's tip

There are a great many poetic features to consider in both poems. In your discussion of the first poem, by Emily Brontë, you would be expected to show a thorough understanding of how the wind becomes personified as a suitor to the poet, and then how this personification allows for further ideas to be expressed towards the end of the poem, particularly ideas about the brevity of human life compared to the eternity of a feature of nature. The mood of the poem, arranged through its formal structure, is peaceful and thoughtful, if slightly mocking and ironic. You might consider whether some of the irony is mocking human beings.

In Hughes' poem you would be expected to deal, at some length, with the violent and disconcerting effect of the storm on human life, and to show how the poet creates a vivid impression of the storm through the use of metaphor, simile, alliteration, assonance and harsh diction. For a fuller answer, the examiner would be interested to see what you make of the more universal idea about human life fearing the natural world, which seems to be contained in the final line.

Once again, you are reminded of the need for a relevant justification of your preference. Possibilities are that you prefer the formal structure of the conversation in *The Night Wind* or the realism of the landscape created by the strident language of *Wind*.

Examiner's comment

We have not interrupted this essay with step by step comments, as we believe it is such a competent and stylish essay as to merit uninterrupted reading. Notice the ease of style with which the candidate writes and the way that she manages to include so many techniques of poetry to show that she is in command of how the poems work.

The subject matter of both poems is an element of nature, namely wind, and this is shown in its contrasting element, softly as in *The Night Wind* and violently as in *Wind*, which is a more modern poem. The fact that each poem is about nature is only half the meaning: each explores a relationship between human life and nature.

In *The Night Wind*, Brontë describes the effects of a whispering, mellow night wind approaching her parlour. This is an idyllic and peaceful scene, as the wind brings with it the scent and glory of summer and then sets her on a course of personifying the wind as a lover. It is also a scene of classical romance as the 'cloudless moon shone through . . .'. At first the wooing of the lover is rejected, and dispatched back to the world of nature:

> 'Play with the scented flower,
> The young tree's supple bough.'

Here she presents herself as the rejecting partner the wind may woo, but she will not succumb easily. The relationship is therefore brought strongly to life. The wooing, however, is persuasive, and its power leads on to an idea of the power in nature, and the contrasting transience and weakness of human life.

In *Wind*, the wind is present as a violent and destructive force, as a storm. Through violent metaphor and simile, the anger and destructiveness of the storm is established and the effect is to drive human beings in on themselves, as if prisoners of nature. Here human beings are overpowered by the wind, left to huddle around a blazing fire for comfort, but reminded of the conflict between human life and nature as they must sit indoors, and hear 'the stones cry out under the horizons'.

The personification in the earlier poem suggests the wind as a sensual and persistent lover, rather mystifying the poet with its charm. Her hair is being softly waved and she is confronted with an intruder of apparent grace and charm:

> 'It told me Heaven was glorious,
> And sleeping Earth was fair.'

It impertinently warns of the menace in its own dark woods, celebrates the great freedom in the spirit of nature: 'Instinct with spirit seem', and even hints at the mystery of its presence as a heavenly element mixing with the earth, in a dream-like state. The wind gains a subtle hold over the poet's emotions, in a sense seducing her, first with its presence and then with its convincing arguments:

> 'Have we not been childhood friends?
> Have I not loved thee long?'

By contrast with the gentleness of personification, the second poem, by Ted Hughes, is built on a series of harsh images, mostly metaphors, which haphazardly and frenetically occur in a freer form of verse. The house is a buffeted boat 'far out at sea all night', the wind a stampeding animal, then replaced in the ensuing calm by the distorted, awkward image of 'the lens of a mad eye'. These have a tone of destructiveness, they are cruel and they all evoke a scene of terrible and awesome discomfort. The strain of the wind in the storm is further developed in the fearful situation of the third verse, which brings in an image of physical torture in the denting of the eyeball and unrelenting pressure in the tautening strain of the tent, an extended metaphor in the last line of this verse.

Hughes uses the freedom of a great deal of enjambement, as if in the same way that the poem sometimes hurries from one line or verse to the next, and is sometimes held back, so too the wind is rushing about the landscape. The eye of the onlooker is visually asked to move quickly from earth to sky and sky to earth:

> 'I dared not once to look up —
> Through the brunt wind that dented the balls of my eyes.'

Compared to Brontë's poem, here there is no unifying spirit of nature in the wind, but instead the elements are unwelcome and become unleashed on the world as a very different kind of force to that used in Brontë's romantic idea. This is one of the interesting things about nature in poetry: how the same element of nature can be presented in contrasting ways. It also reminds the reader that nature can be interpreted as both friend and enemy. Hughes uses alliteration to suggest the unwanted power of the wind:

> 'The hills had new places, and wind wielded
> Blade-light, luminous and emerald.'

This all to me evokes the idea of the wind having a mind of its own, and a mind that is dangerous and lethal, so much so that there is even destruction in its wake of other elements of nature: the 'black-/Back gull bent like an iron bar slowly'. This destruction is tortuous, cruel and even tyrannical.

The conclusion is that, as if in some kind of battle, human life is imprisoned, but even when people hide away from the wind, there is no solace, no comfort in withdrawing from the violent world of nature:

> '. . . Now deep
> In chairs, in front of the great fire, we grip
> Our hearts . . .'

The wind will just not leave them alone. The poem then becomes sinister in the final line, which suggests that human life remains at the mercy of nature:

> 'Hearing the stones cry out under the horizons.'

In the final verse a strong visual scene is created of the human beings living at the mercy of the elements. I find this is particularly well created by the separate phrase 'but sit on', which conjures up a scene of an eternal nightmare indoors at the horror of the wind outside. It is very effective at strengthening the main theme in the poem, which seems to be the terror of people at the hands of brutal elements of nature.

In *The Night Wind*, there is much more of a concluding meaning. Emily Brontë has given the wind a voice throughout, as if a character as well as a presence. The idea argued by this character, the wind, is that life is a mere fleeting presence, a temporary state, always close to its end. This sense of invincibility can be compared to the eternal spirit of nature: 'I shall have time enough to mourn'.

Emotion is also expressed for both 'lovers' — a pathos for the wind, and loneliness for the poet, possibly even suggesting for the poet a kind of morbid feeling, a fear of her own death in the rather lamentable and lyrical lines:

> 'And when thy heart is laid at rest
> Beneath the church-yard stone . . .'

Is there also a rebuke for the poet's arrogant human attitude? This could form the meanings of the final three verses, when, after hearing the rebuttal of the poet's voice in the sixth verse, the wind becomes impatient and tells her:

> 'I'll win thee 'gainst thy will.'

Then the wind continues to become impatient, reminding her of her mortality.

It is difficult to judge, as I have enjoyed both poems. Of the two, I am less convinced by Hughes' poem, although I find it very skilfully written, especially the imagery, which matches the violence, and the sound patterns which have a similar effect. Although it presents a vivid and detailed picture which can be recognised, and which is both exciting and disturbing, I altogether prefer the odd idea of the use of the wind as a character who becomes a kind of lover in Brontë's poem. I found I had to work harder for the concluding idea, and this

made the conclusion all the stronger. In the end, the poem was not all romantic, but had warnings in it of the imminence of death for all human beings, compared with nature. I liked the way that the cleverness of the poem worked in a kind of fantasy situation set against a backdrop of reality:

> 'A cloudless moon shone through
> Our open parlour window.'

Finally, I also have to admit that I enjoyed the beauty of *The Night Wind* more than the harshness of *Wind*, even though that poem may have been more realistic in a sense.

Examiner's comment

Clearly a very skilful candidate, able to integrate meaning and technique at a very high level. It is good to see so much close reference. We liked the enthusiasm and respect for the work of the poets, and this was evident in the polite way that the candidate extolled the virtues of both poems before stating her preference for Brontë. The argument for the preference was a very good one, the only disappointment being her unwillingness to extend her perfectly valid point at the end about the greater beauty of the earlier poem. Here was perhaps an opportunity to write something about the contrast between formal and free verse — she might, for example, have commented upon the rhyming pattern in *The Night Wind*, although to be fair she competently dealt with the effects of enjambement in Hughes' poem.

What this essay shows above all else are the advantages of developing your own style of writing, which here was highly sophisticated, and also of expressing an enthusiasm for poetry, which came across throughout.

3 *Prose*

In the appreciations you write about prose extracts, you will particularly need to:

- identify the main elements of the prose (narrative/descriptive/didactic etc.);
- comment on the writers' attitudes to the subject matter;
- deal with characterisation;
- analyse the ways in which locations play their part in the meanings;
- interpret the use of dialogue;
- show how writers arrange their works in order to create such features as irony, tension, suspense, humour, etc;
- bring out realism and comment on the purpose of close description;
- show how the pace of a passage will be able to contribute to its overall effect.

A ANALYSING A SINGLE WRITING STYLE

Read carefully the following passage, which is taken from *Mary Barton* by Elizabeth Gaskell (1848). The book is a study of the hardships of working life in the mid-nineteenth century, set mainly in Manchester. In this passage, the author is describing the problems facing a character recently made unemployed due to the failure and closure of a local mill.

Write an appreciation of the passage, bringing out ways in which the style of the writing contributes to your understanding of the plight of the character. You should also comment on the ways in which the attitudes of the writer towards her subject are established.

Mary Barton

But there are earnest men among these people, men who have endured wrongs without complaining, but without ever forgetting or forgiving those whom (they believe) have caused all this woe.

Among these was John Barton. His parents had suffered, his mother had died from absolute want of the necessities of life. He himself was a good, steady workman, and, as such, pretty certain of steady employment. But he spent all he got with the confidence (you may also call it improvidence) of one who was willing, and believed himself able, to supply all his wants by his own exertions. And when his master suddenly failed, and all hands in that mill were turned back, one Tuesday morning, with the news that Mr Hunter had stopped, Barton had only a few shillings to rely on; but he had a good heart of being employed at some other mill, and accordingly, before returning home, he spent some hours in going from factory to factory, asking for work. But at every mill was some sign of depression of trade; some were working short hours, some were turning off hands, and for weeks Barton was out of work, living on credit. It was during this time his little son, the apple of his eye, the cynosure of all his strong power of love, fell ill of the scarlet fever. They dragged him through the crisis, but his life hung on a gossamer thread. Everything, the doctor said, depended on good nourishment, on generous living, to keep up the little fellow's strength, in the prostration in which the fever had left him. Mocking words! when the commonest food in the house would not furnish one little meal. Barton tried credit; but it was worn out at the little provision shops, which were now suffering in their turn. He thought it would be no sin to steal, and would have stolen; but he could not get the opportunity in the few days the child lingered. Hungry himself, almost to an animal pitch of ravenousness, but with the bodily pain swallowed up in anxiety for his little sinking lad, he stood at one of the shop windows where all edible luxuries were displayed;

38

haunches of venison, Stilton cheeses, moulds of jelly — all appetising sights to the common passer by. And out of this shop came Mrs Hunter! She crossed to her carriage, followed by the shopman, loaded with purchases for a party. The door was quickly slammed to, and she drove away; and Barton returned home with a bitter spirit of wrath in his heart, to see his only boy a corpse!

You can fancy, now, the hoards of vengeance in his heart against the employers. For there are never wanting those who, either in speech or in print, find it in their interest to cherish such feelings in the working classes; who know how and when to rouse the dangerous power at their command; and who use their knowledge with unrelenting purpose to either party.

ELIZABETH GASKELL

Examiner's tip

When you are asked to appreciate a single prose passage you need to write in a lot more detail than you might do for a comparison, when you would need to be more selective.

An examiner would be interested to see how well you manage to bring out the desperate predicament of the character (especially in terms of his hunger and the effects on his family) by analysing the style, which is disturbing and plain-speaking, without ever being elaborate or over-dramatic.

With regard to the writer's attitudes, an examiner will want to assess how well you have pointed to features of diction, to some of the contrasts in the descriptions of life, and how well you have coped with the engagement of the narrator's voice in the passage to bring out the tragedy and hardship of the situation. There does seem to be a relationship established between the narrator and the reader, and it would be essential to show how this is brought about, and what it tells us about Elizabeth Gaskell's views of her subject.

ANSWER

Gaskell manages to achieve an impression of suffering throughout the passage. There is a depressive tone and aspects of the actions are unfeeling. There is an unpleasant, desperate air to the life of John Barton, compounded by the fact that it has been so with his parents: 'His parents had suffered' — thus neither generation were well off and neither had found any comfort. It is also evident that the author's views seep through the life of John Barton: 'You can fancy, now, the hoards of vengeance in his heart against the employers.' This seems to involve the author, and so we sympathise with the character, but also realise that it is a joint view: it is also Elizabeth Gaskell's view. She and her character become one, and she suffers with him.

Examiner's comment

It is impressive that the candidate has been willing, so soon at the start of the essay, to deal with the way that the writer involves herself with the central character.

It is the author's style which helps the reader in many ways to comprehend the suffering of John Barton. The most obvious technique is that the content of the passage focuses on the effects on the family. This makes the events realistic, and we as readers can respond to the plight and conditions of this poor working family. Gaskell helps us to feel empathy towards the entire family, and not just John. There is a strong emotional tone in the way that she describes his son; 'his little son, the apple of his eye'. We are led to feel the suffering of the rest of the family, which will be affected by the result of John's unemployment.

The love and responsibility that John Barton feels for his family is expressed in strong terms. The diction chosen helps the reader to understand his love for family and child. John himself puts his family first: 'Hungry himself', but that hunger was 'swallowed up in anxiety for his little sinking lad'. The choice of such language as 'swallowed' and 'sinking' strikes the reader with the awful truth of suffering in this situation. It is very direct. Gaskell attempts to make her reader know exactly her character's emotional state without any irony or satire. She is honest and frank — her words can be taken literally to depict the plain fact that John Barton has no choice in life, his conditions cause him to suffer, but he will do everything for his poor family. This disperses the sympathy that we are engaged in feeling. It is sympathy deflected onto the plight of the family. He is desperate to help his family survive: 'before returning home, he spent some hours . . .'. There is pride and determination in this man of love and care, all of which Gaskell conveys in a very positive manner.

Examiner's comment

There is a lot contained in this paragraph, which is impressive. What we like is the way that the candidate combines so effectively a discussion of the character, which is one of the main focal points in the rubric of the question, with a consideration of language, especially the point about diction.

The seriousness of the situation is emphasised by the death of the child, but this death is never over-dramatised. We know how fond Barton is of his son, and how affected he would be by his death. We are prepared for this, and we also admire the way that he has trudged around from mill to mill in search of work. When the death is described it is conveyed such that perhaps the reader should not dwell on the death, but on what caused it: 'Barton returned home with a bitter spirit of wrath in his heart, to see his only boy a corpse!' The death made up only a short part of the passage, but as a reader I was inclined to ask such questions as: Was it poverty? How bad was the illness? The child's suffering is expressed earlier in the passage in the sad statement: 'his life hung on a gossamer thread'. The central focus on the death, and the way that it is slightly understated — almost as an anti-climax to the incident when Mrs Hunter, contrastingly, leaves the shop with her arms full of plentiful provisions, makes the passage extremely depressing in its nature. The reader can be in no doubt as to the anger and bitterness felt by Barton, and by Elizabeth Gaskell, at the awful poverty and desperation of the family.

Examiner's comment

Excellent progression. We like the way that reference is being made to points in the passage which prepare the reader for the child's death, and also the contrasts that are brought out. He is also able to show something of the relationship between the author and the reader, which is an important skill.

Gaskell's own opinions are conveyed to the reader very plainly. One of the major ways is in the direct contrast between the quality of life of rich and poor. She has no reservations in making her opinions felt about the richer mill-owners. Barton's dismissal is dealt with in a way that suggests that he is unlucky and has no control over his life. The mill hands were turned back 'one Tuesday morning', and the way that this is written makes the time seem very insignificant, as if the mill could have failed at any time. This makes Barton's problems appear like chance, as if he had no say in the matter and was out of control of his own fate.

There may even be a hint of irony in the phrase 'his master suddenly failed', as it appears anything but a sudden decision.

However, the main difference between the two classes is highlighted through food: 'edible luxuries were displayed; haunches of venison, Stilton cheeses, moulds of jelly . . . The door was quickly slammed to.' Here we feel sympathy directly for Barton as it is as if the food is all on offer — it is an enticing part of the prose — and then we suffer, with him, his torment of disappointment and denial, as it is impossible for him to afford such luxuries.

Examiner's comment

We like the capacity in this candidate to find examples from the text and to analyse them in some depth. There is a confident feeling that he is choosing his examples for a purpose, rather than simply quoting indiscriminately.

In my opinion, the entire tone of the passage asks for sympathy towards Barton's position. The author merges skills of persuasion with strong attitudes against the way that the working classes are treated so harshly. These persuasive skills come through direct writing which is calmly but insistently descriptive of his situation, and which involves her, as the author, stating her point of view occasionally in a disbelieving way: 'Mocking words! when the commonest food in the house would not furnish one little meal'. It is almost as if Gaskell is observing the social situation and documenting it, and her writing is trying to convince her that these awful things are happening.

Following all the terrible events: his being laid off, no other employment to be found, the hunger, and most strongly, the death of his loved son, the tempo is increased at the end of this extract, with a strong feeling that the working classes will *do* something about their situation. The reader can sympathise with this by the end because of the way that Gaskell has incorporated her skills of persuasion with her expression of attitudes against the upper classes. The result is a well-structured and very moving passage.

Examiner's comment

The essay finishes with a genuine conclusion, coming back to the point, in the penultimate paragraph, about the style and the author's intentions, a helpful reminder to the examiner that the candidate has remained mindful of the requirements of the question. The only critical point we have is that there might have been a stronger analysis of the final paragraph, which does contain some important ideas. Undoubtedly, when the passage was set, the examiners would have had in mind the need to consider the difficult ideas contained in the final paragraph, as they are slightly more complex and general than the situation which has been described earlier. But all things considered, this is a fine answer, showing awareness of the style and attitudes. There is a strong sense of commitment from the candidate, which does him no harm, and his own organisation is excellent.

B COMPARING THE OPENINGS OF TWO NOVELS

Many writers attempt to engage the interest of their readers with the use of dramatic openings to novels or short stories. This is attempted in the two examples that follow: the openings to *The Virgin and the Gipsy* by D H Lawrence (1930) and *Brighton Rock* by Graham Greene (1938). Comment on the varying styles used by these two writers and state whether they have been successful in creating dramatic openings to their respective works. Which passage strikes you as more successful?

(a)

The Virgin and the Gipsy

When the vicar's wife went off with a young and penniless man the scandal knew no bounds. Her two little girls were only seven and nine years old respectively. And the vicar was such a good husband. True, his hair was grey. But his moustache was dark, he was handsome, and still full of furtive passion for his unrestrained and beautiful wife.

Why did she go? Why did she burst away with such an *éclat* of revulsion, like a touch of madness?

Nobody gave any answer. Only the pious said she was a bad woman. While some of the good women kept silent. They knew.

The two little girls never knew. Wounded, they decided that it was because their mother found them negligible.

The ill wind that blows nobody any good swept away the vicarage family on its blast. Then lo and behold! the vicar, who was somewhat distinguished as an essayist and controversialist, and whose case had aroused sympathy among the bookish men, received the living of Papplewick. The Lord had tempered the wind of misfortune with a rectorate in the north country.

The rectory was a rather ugly stone house down by the river Papple, before you come into the village. Further on, beyond where the road crosses the stream, were the big old stone cotton-mills, once driven by water. The road curved up-hill, into the bleak stone streets of the village.

The vicarage family received decided modification, upon its transference into the rectory. The vicar, now the rector, fetched up his old mother and his sister, and a brother from the city. The two little girls had a very different milieu from the old home.

D H LAWRENCE

(b)

Brighton Rock

Hale knew, before he had been in Brighton three hours, that they meant to murder him. With his inky fingers and his bitten nails, his manner cynical and nervous, anybody could tell he didn't belong — belong to the early summer sun, the cool Whitsun wind off the sea, the holiday crowd. They came in by train from Victoria every five minutes, rocked down Queen's Road standing on the tops of the little local trams, stepped off in bewildered multitudes into fresh and glittering air: the new silver paint sparkled on the piers, the cream houses ran away into the west like a pale Victorian water-colour; a race in miniature motors, a band playing, flower gardens in bloom below the front, an aeroplane advertising something for the health in pale vanishing clouds across the sky.

It had seemed quite easy to Hale to be lost in Brighton. Fifty thousand people besides himself were down here for the day, and for quite a while he gave himself up to the good day, drinking gins and tonics wherever his programme allowed. For he had to stick closely to a programme: from ten till eleven Queen's Road and Castle Square, from eleven till twelve the Aquarium and Palace Pier, twelve till one the front between the Old Ship and West Pier, back for lunch between one and two in any restaurant he chose round Castle Square, and after that he had to make his way all down the parade to the West Pier and then to the station by the Hove streets. These were the limits of his absurd and widely advertised sentry-go.

Advertised on every *Messenger* poster: 'Kolley Kibber in Brighton today.' In his pocket he had a packet of cards to distribute in hidden places along his route; those who found them would receive ten shillings from the *Messenger*, but the big prize was reserved for whoever challenged Hale in the proper form of words and with a copy of the Messenger in his hand: 'You are Mr Kolley Kibber. I claim the *Daily Messenger* prize.'

GRAHAM GREENE

Examiner's tip

There are a number of features that a good answer might refer to in this question. Both passages establish situations which form elements of intrigue from which the stories can develop, and these, a feature of the action, should be commented upon. In terms of action or situation, both passages also rely on the probability of further important events emanating from the initial dramatic points: the new family life and living for the girls in Lawrence's novel and the fear of murder and the Kolley Kibber identification in the passage from Graham Greene.

The examiner will be interested to see how well you compare the two styles: the painful, emotional style from Lawrence compared with the packed, eventful and tense style of Greene's writing which is reminiscent of a murder mystery.

Although Lawrence does so more explicitly than Greene, both openings raise questions: what will happen to the girls in their new abode of the Papplewick Vicarage? Will Hale be confronted, discovered or murdered?

In terms of specific comparisons of style, there would need to be recognition of Lawrence's more open, discursive, even informal style in the first passage, which contains some strong emotional features, and the terse, relentless, highly charged and detailed description of scene and action which characterises Greene's style.

Do not forget to state a preference. Relevant reasons for your choice might be: a preference for establishing a mystery, for the engagement of emotions, or for the capacity of one writer to create a realistic opening.

ANSWER

The opening sentence of *The Virgin and the Gipsy* is immediately engaging as Lawrence informs the reader of recent scandalous events. His subject of the 'vicar's wife' defying her respectable social role by eloping with a 'young and penniless man' is shocking, and we are made aware of the repercussions of this incident as 'the scandal knew no bounds', a matter upon which the author subsequently enlarges by carefully introducing the 'two little girls'. Here the diction is important to the power of the passage. Choice of words such as 'little' and 'only' serve to magnify the severity of the mother's hasty departure, and our sympathy for 'the good husband' is heightened. He is next to be described.

There is a speculative tone to the description of the vicar, as denoted by the openings to each sentence ('And', 'True', 'But'). Lawrence's style is deliberately meant to suggest the probable gossip surrounding the elopement and the enticing nature of the scandal, which is further marked by the questioning in the second paragraph: 'Why did she go . . . Why did she burst away . . ?' Naturally the reader wants to know how and why the 'beautiful wife' abandoned her seemingly ideal family. The word 'beautiful' in this phrase surely becomes ironic. As we read on Lawrence suggests a contradiction. First of all we read 'Nobody gave any answer', but then, in a knowing and emotional way, perhaps evoking the sadness of the desertion: 'They knew'. Furthermore, Lawrence again invokes our sympathy by returning to the presence of the innocent victims — the 'two little girls'. This is accomplished with a style which is heart-rending and disturbing: 'Wounded, they decided that it was because their mother found them negligible.'

However, Lawrence is most successful in encouraging the reader to continue when he informs us of the next stage of the vicar's family life, which is to take place at Papplewick. We assume that the details of the mystery about the mother's departure will be revealed at a later stage in the novel, and he has seemingly deflected from its source for the time being. Yet such a digression does not lessen the impact of the opening. The character of the vicar is developed and our attention is drawn to him. We are told that this husband of the adulteress was 'somewhat distinguished as an essayist and controversialist'. He too must therefore warrant close attention, especially as we are constantly reminded of this misfortune. Through a tentative opening, Lawrence has started off a number of threads

---

about the characters, including the children, and so we are curious to read on and discover about their lives and problems.

The opening sentence of *Brighton Rock* is equally engaging but in a more dramatic way, from the tradition of a novel which deals with the reality of violence and crime in modern life. Whereas there is a degree of scandal to shock the reader of Lawrence's book, here the reader is immediately drawn into murder, mystery and intrigue. Hale is a stranger, a misfit, and questions are raised through a description of his actions and through the tone of the passage, about his whole being and purpose.

The reader wants to know why he is in Brighton, and even more importantly, why does he know that people want to murder him? The style of this passage is varied. The intense drama of the opening is dispensed with as Greene slows down the pace with some description. This description of the holidaymakers and the traditional, friendly scene at the seaside is a relief for a short while from the dramatic tension of Hale's plight and fate. It is even quite a poetic, romantic and idyllic scene: 'bands playing, flower gardens in bloom below the front'. The reader is given a few moments of pleasure in reading about this scene before returning to the sordid reality of Hale's worries, and clearly the contrast is intended to heighten the problems of the character. Indeed, there is a marked and deliberate contrast between the scene of the holiday resort and Hale: the two are totally different entities. But then Greene brings together Hale and the seaside location. He becomes part of the scene, and the pace picks up again as we learn that Hale is sticking very closely to a rigid pattern: 'For he had to stick closely to a programme'. This leads the reader down a path of questioning why he has to stick to a 'programme', and what the programme can be. The way the word is used gives it a sinister connotation.

The mood then changes again in the third paragraph. The importance of the timings described in the second has been able to build up a picture of the character's mysterious actions. (Why have these locations been important for him? Who is observing him?) Now the timings have finished and confusion sets in: 'Advertised on every Messenger poster: "Kolley Kibber in Brighton today".' We begin to wonder, through the mysterious questioning technique, whether in fact Hale and Kolley Kibber are one and the same person. And if they are not then the style of the passage builds up a fascination with the outcome, like a mystery thriller.

Greene confuses his readers and raises this series of questions for them, encouraging them to read on in order to satisfy curiosity awakened by the deliberately obtuse opening. There are a number of themes which are hinted at, e.g. murder, violence in the modern world, and mysterious actions (the cards that had to be distributed, the business about the Messenger) — and they provide a powerful opening view of what the book might be about later.

In my opinion, Greene's is the more successful style. Lawrence allows the reader to speculate on the emotions of the characters, but Greene is more powerful. I would want to continue *Brighton Rock* because I imagine that the text to follow would be unpredictable and mysterious, and in a way it is therefore more gripping. The opening threatens an exciting and intriguing plot, whereas Lawrence tempts the reader to follow the fortunes of his characters in more of an emotional way. I also prefer the way that Greene manages to combine two different styles of writing: mysterious and realistic. I get the impression that this will be a story of suspense, but that it will reflect some violent truths about society.

C   COMPARING TWO EXTRACTS OF MODERN PROSE

The following extracts express, in different ways, a similar theme. Compare the passages, commenting on the techniques used by each writer to bring out the theme of loneliness.

Extracts from *The Heart of the Matter*, by Graham Greene (1948) and *The Battle Lost and Won*, Volume Two of *The Levant Trilogy* by Olivia Manning (1978).

(a)   *The Heart of the Matter*

EXTRACT

Wilson sat on the balcony of the Bedford Hotel with his bald pink knees thrust against the ironwork. It was Sunday and the Cathedral bell clanged for matins. On the other side of Bond Street, in the windows of the High School, sat the young negresses in dark blue gym smocks engaged in the interminable task of trying to wave their wirespring hair. Wilson stroked his very young moustache and dreamed, waiting for his gin-and-bitters.

Sitting there, facing Bond Street, he had his face turned to the sea. His pallor showed how recently he had emerged from it into the port: so did his lack of interest in the schoolgirls opposite. He was like the lagging finger of the barometer, still pointing to Fair long after its companion had moved to Stormy. Below him the black clerks moved churchward, but their wives in brilliant afternoon dresses of blue and cerise aroused no interest in Wilson. He was alone on the balcony except for one bearded Indian in a turban who had already tried to tell his fortune: this was not the hour or the day for white men — they would be at the beach five miles away, but Wilson had no car. He felt almost intolerably lonely. On either side of the school the tin roofs sloped toward the sea, and the corrugated iron above his head clanged and clattered as a vulture alighted.

GRAHAM GREENE

(b)   *The Levant Trilogy*

EXTRACT

Simon Boulderstone, coming into Cairo on leave, passed the pyramids at Giza when they were hazed over by mid-day heat. The first time he had seen them, he had been struck with wonder, but now there was no wonder left in the world. His brother, Hugo, had been killed. That very morning, in the dark, early hours, Hugo had bled to death in no-man's-land.

Simon had stopped a lorry on the coast road east of Alamein and, alone in the back, had cried himself to sleep. Now that he would have to face the two men in front, he tried to wipe away the marks of tears but did not do it very well. The lorry stopped outside the Mena House. The driver, coming round to speak to Simon, stared at him, then said, 'You've caught the sun, sir,' as though they had not, all of them, been broiled by sun during the long summer months.

'You want anywhere in particular, sir?'

'A cheap hotel, if you know of one.'

The driver suggested the International, and Simon said, 'Glad if you'd drop me there.' They drove on through the suburbs into the centre of Cairo where the lorry stopped again. They were at a modern Midan, a meeting place of three small streets where the old houses were being pulled down and replaced by concrete blocks. One of the blocks was the International and it had the unadorned air of cheapness.

Throwing down his kit, Simon thanked the two men then jumped down himself. Standing on the pavement, in the dazzling light, he seemed to be in a trance, and the driver asked him: 'You all right, sir?'

Simon nodded and the lorry went on. Left alone in the middle of the Midan, he stared at a palm tree that rose from a bed of ashy sand. As he observed it, he began to feel an extraordinary poignancy about it so for a few minutes he could not move, but, forgetting Hugo, he centred his misery on this solitary palm. From its height and the length of its fronds, he could guess it was an old tree that had grown in other, more spacious days. Now, seeing it hemmed in by buildings like a bird in too small a cage, he ached with pity for it though the tree itself conveyed no sense of deprivation. A human being in a similar case would have been bemoaning his misfortune, but the tree, swaying in the hot wind, spread itself as though rejoicing in such air and light as came to it.

OLIVIA MANNING

Examiner's tip

There are similarities between these passages, and there would need to be recognition of these similarities. Both passages are given exotic settings and both study the situation of a character who is alienated by those exotic settings, Wilson apparently through his intolerable loneliness and Simon Boulderstone through personal tragedy. The examiner would be interested to read what you make of the settings, including the climate, and how well you connect the locations with the moods and situations of the two central characters. Indeed, both passages are fine examples of the way that detail, when being used to create a sense of place, can have a bearing on meaning and characterisation.

In terms of differences, you might be expected to show an understanding of the way that Greene's style highlights intense personal feelings of discomfort, often quite directly, whereas Manning appears to create the pathos much more through a narration of the situation. You would be expected to show how Manning's style distances the main character from the world continuing around him.

Be prepared to refer to specific instances of style, such as Greene's striking imagery and Manning's powerful symbolism towards the end of the extract.

Both passages are extracted from a tradition of literature which is intensely British: about British citizens serving abroad. These settings allowed many twentieth century writers to express grief and human tragedy in distant settings of realism. At the very least, you ought to refer to the realism.

Because there is no requirement for a preference, you are advised not to make one.

ANSWER

In the two passages studied, there are some similarities in the techniques used to bring out the theme of loneliness.

To begin with, both passages are written in the third person, which means that we can read them from an independent, even distant, point of view. Had they been written in the first person we would know of the feelings more directly, we would know the exact feelings personally. Here, in both instances we are either told how the characters feel or we realise the feelings through their circumstances.

The main characters in the extracts; Wilson in the first passage and Simon in the second, are both young: 'Wilson stroked his very young moustache.' and Simon, we know, 'had cried himself to sleep.' Loneliness, we sense, is therefore all the more harsh. Both characters have also made journeys alone, and are staying, isolated, in hotels abroad. Simon, it is stressed, is staying in a 'cheap' hotel, without the luxury of comfort, and to add to the isolation of Wilson, we hear that he is in a sordid environment.

Wilson's discomfort and feelings of loneliness are possibly compounded by racial discomfort. He is a white man alone in a black community. He is 'alone on the balcony except for one bearded Indian'. Then we learn that 'this was not the hour or the day for white men — they would be at the beach five miles away'. Clearly this adds to the feeling established in the passage anyway that he cannot relate to his surroundings, nor to the people in them. There is also mention of Sunday and 'matins'. The streets around him seem deserted, and this provides a contrast with the noise of the church bells and the announcement of morning service. Alone, on a Sunday, up early in the morning, aware of all around him going to church, distracted by the sight of the young negresses in their dark blue gym smocks, he becomes acutely aware of his situation. The writer stresses this through the references to the activities of the other, local people, around him, and the people going to church:

'Below him the black clerks moved churchward'

It may have been that the worship in the church was meant to signify a sense of community. Wilson was not part of this community; he was looking at it from the outside, and it is this which stresses his acute sense of loneliness.

Another instance of the feeling of being left behind is in the image of the barometer. In this simile, he is 'like the lagging finger . . . pointing to Fair long after its companion had moved to Stormy'. This is a strong image and gives us the impression of Wilson having been deserted. Even if he has not actually been deserted, e.g. by a friend, we can sense his being left out by other human beings. From this simile we even begin to sense a characterisation of Wilson which suggests not just that this is a lonely situation for him here, but that he is a loner by personality.

Finally, Greene uses a vulture to help symbolise Wilson's loneliness. Vultures fly by themselves and only come together when they can scavenge food. Also, the vulture introduces a tone of violence and destruction to the passage, giving it overall a mood of foreboding.

In the second passage, time of day is also important. In just the same way that Wilson's loneliness is confirmed and expressed by the early morning, so here the heat of midday is important. Simon Boulderstone is passing the pyramids during the midday heat, which is presumably a time of siesta.

Simon's brother had been killed and had 'bled to death in no-man's-land'. The interesting thing about this, apart from the grief felt by Simon, is the transfer of the theme and mood of loneliness onto the agony of the brother's death. The impression of no-man's-land is a solitary place where no one else would venture. Added to this is the terrible distance that Simon feels from his brother — death is final and I get the impression that he is stunned by it as a result. Thus, he is, at this point, at his loneliest state.

As is the time, so the climate is also alienating him. It is difficult to feel at home or at ease when the heat is so stifling: 'Standing . . . in the dazzling light, he seemed to be in a trance . . .'. The emotional language that Manning uses constantly expresses alienation and loneliness, for example: 'Left alone . . . centred his misery . . . solitary palm . . .'. From the description of the 'solitary palm', there was a time when it grew with other trees. Like the tree, there was a time when Simon was with other people, including his brother. Manning stresses the strength in the tree's life, and now this contrasts with the awful numbing grief felt by Simon at the death of his brother, in this alien environment.

Manning uses the dialogue quite effectively, again to emphasise Simon's loneliness. This is rather different to Greene's passage which in other ways is more descriptive of Wilson's condition. The tone of the speech used by the driver is courteous, as if he does not want to disturb Simon's private grief:

'The driver . . . then said, "You've caught the sun, sir," as though they had not, all of them, been broiled by sun during the long summer months.'

Then, later, there is a tone of tenderness in the way the driver asks him if he is all right.

Both passages use similar descriptive techniques to describe the lonely surroundings. In the first passage it is easy to imagine the scene, which is rather run down and sordid, through the girls sitting casually in the High School windows and the tin roofs sloping down towards the sea. In Manning's passage there is a disturbing feeling of modern concrete urban life taking over the mood as Simon arrives at the hotel: 'old houses were being pulled down and replaced by concrete blocks'.

Examiner's comment

The essay continues well, structuring the discussion of the second passage in the same way as the first. It is pleasing to see the candidate handle the three issues of symbolism, dialogue and description, and it is also reassuring that she is able to refer back to the first passage at an important and relevant point in her discussion.

The overall picture of the two passages seems to be of lonely young men who have suffered different experiences to cause their loneliness, and vivid descriptions are used to show the alienation of the two men.

Examiner's comment

Conclusions are difficult, and this one does not, frankly, add a great deal to the passage. It rather states the obvious in our view, and the candidate may have preferred to make a final comparative point between the styles of the passages or the situations of the characters.
    Overall, the structure of the essay is commendable, stylistically sound if not resoundingly elegant, and always relevant.

D COMPARING STYLE AND EFFECTIVENESS IN TWO PROSE PASSAGES

The following extracts focus on dramatic incidents with horses: *Tess of the d'Urbervilles* by Thomas Hardy (1892) and *Women in Love* by D H Lawrence (1920). Compare the passages in the following ways:

(a) How does the style of the writing express the drama of each incident?

(b) How successfully do the writers express the feelings and responses of the characters to the events?

(c) Which passage strikes you as more dramatically effective?

(a)   *Tess of the d'Urbervilles*

EXTRACT

The lantern hanging at her waggon had gone out, but another was shining in her face — much brighter than her own had been. Something terrible had happened. The harness was entangled with an object which blocked the way.

In consternation Tess jumped down, and discovered the dreadful truth. The groan had proceeded from her father's poor horse Prince. The morning mailcart, with its two noiseless wheels, speeding along these lanes like an arrow, as it always did, had driven into her slow and unlighted equipage. The pointed shaft of the cart had entered the breast of the unhappy Prince like a sword, and from the wound his life's blood was spouting in a stream, and falling with a hiss into the road.

In her despair Tess sprang forward and put her hand upon the hole, with the only result that she became splashed from face to skirt with the crimson drops. Then she stood helplessly looking on. Prince also stood firm and motionless as long as he could; till he suddenly sank down in a heap.

By this time the mail-cart man had joined her, and began dragging and unharnessing the hot form of Prince. But he was already dead, and, seeing nothing more could be done immediately, the mail-cart man returned to his own animal, which was uninjured.

'You was on the wrong side,' he said. 'I am bound to go on with the mail-bags, so that the best thing for you to do is to bide here with your load. I'll send somebody to help you as soon as I can. It is getting daylight, and you have nothing to fear.'

He mounted and sped on his way; while Tess stood and waited. The atmosphere turned pale, the birds shook themselves in the hedges, arose, and twittered; the lane showed all its white features, and Tess showed hers, still whiter. The huge pool of blood in front of her was already assuming the iridescence of coagulation; and when the sun rose a hundred prismatic hues were reflected in it. Prince lay alongside still and stark; his eyes half open, the hole in his chest looking scarcely large enough to have let out all that had animated him.

'Tis all my doing — all mine!' the girl cried, gazing at the spectacle. 'No excuse for me — none. What will mother and father live on now? Aby, Aby!' She shook the child, who had slept soundly through the whole disaster. 'We can't go on with our load — Prince is killed!'

THOMAS HARDY

EXTRACT *(b)*

Women in Love

'The fool!' cried Ursula loudly. 'Why doesn't he ride away till it's gone by?'

Gudrun was looking at him with black-dilated, spellbound eyes. But he sat glistening and obstinate, forcing the wheeling mare, which spun and swerved like a wind, and yet could not get out of the grasp of his will, nor escape from the mad clamour of terror that resounded through her, as the trucks thumped slowly, heavily, horrifyingly, one after the other, one pursuing the other, over the rails of the crossing.

The locomotive, as if wanting to see what could be done, put on the brakes, and back came the trucks rebounding on the iron buffers, striking like horrible cymbals, clashing nearer and nearer in frightful strident concussions. The mare opened her mouth and rose slowly, as if lifted up on a wind of terror. Then suddenly her forefeet struck out, as she convulsed herself utterly away from the horror. Back she went, and the two girls clung to each other, feeling she must fall backwards on top of him. But he leaned forward, his face shining with fixed amusement, and at last he brought her down, sank her down, and was bearing her back to the mark. But as strong as the pressure of his compulsion was the repulsion of her utter terror, throwing her back away from the railway, so that she spun round and round on two legs, as if she were in the centre of some whirlwind. It made Gudrun faint with poignant dizziness, which seemed to penetrate her heart.

D H LAWRENCE

> **Examiner's tip**
>
> In this type of task, you are asked quite specifically to answer certain stated questions. As examiners, we would prefer to read replies in which the answers to all three questions have been integrated into one essay — mainly because this is better style at A-level. However, separate answers are acceptable, provided they are presented in the form of critical appreciation and provided all the ground is covered.
>
> An examiner would be looking for evidence of a contrast in the dramatic styles: above all the pitiful and lamentable detailed narrative account of events in Hardy's passage against the startling and shocking style which is a feature of Lawrence's writing.
>
> The tone of pathos and the sense of vulnerability and fatalistic despair of the character from *Tess of the D'Urbervilles* could be contrasted with the variety of moods (terror and violence amongst them) of the characters in the extract from *Women in Love*.
>
> In all parts of your answer, reference to the imagery and the personification, perhaps even to symbolism, would be helpful for a complete answer, as would reference to the pace dictated by the form of sentence structure
>
> There is a direct request for a preference. Remember the points about making this part of your answer relevant: you need to show how the style and tone of the writing makes your preferred passage more dramatic.

ANSWER

In the passage from *Women in Love*, the dramatic effect is portrayed on a surface level by the extensive use of imagery. The constant references to spinning, dizziness and concussion suggest that the situation is out of control and that the characters are panicking: they must wait until the situation has played itself out. The scene is about an incident in which a horse is frightened by the noise of a train, and Lawrence's repetition of the words 'horror' and 'terror' make the fear of the incident intensely real and distressing to the reader. Phrases such as 'the mad clamour of terror' and 'frightful strident concussions' intensify the fear of the horse and the women.

There is a suggestion in the tone of description of both the train and the horse, that their respective violent movements express the strong feelings that Gudrun has for the character on the horse, especially as we are given some ideas about her feelings for this man from the way she is looking at him in the second paragraph. Then we learn about the strength of feeling, physically, in the horse, who:

> 'could not get out of the grasp of his will, nor escape from the mad clamour of terror that resounded through her'

The locomotive is personified and given a strongly prominent violence in its movements, which complements the feelings of the woman and also reflects back the strength of the horse, and as a consequence there is a lot of unity in the style and structure of this writing:

> 'The locomotive, as if wanting to see what could be done, put on the brakes'

In a continuation of this personification, the imagery becomes equally strident:

> 'striking like horrible cymbals . . .'

This personification gives the passage an unusual perspective as the incident can be seen from the point of view of everyone and everything involved, not just from the characters'. This is the effect of the symbolism: all parts represent the sudden situation and mood, the characters, the horse and the engine. There is also a feeling of being trapped that occurs from the rider controlling the horse. The animal is terrified and keeps trying to escape, but is continually 'brought down' or 'sank down' by her rider, who is struggling to gain control. This sensation also adds to the feeling of chaos brought about by the startling language.

As well as the violent personification and violent imagery, Lawrence plays a great deal with the sounds of words, using the effect of onomatopoeia to good purpose (the trucks which 'thumped slowly' are 'clashing' in the third paragraph.)

Examiner's comment

It is slightly odd that the discussion of the second passage should come first, but this is probably because there is going to be preference stated later for the Hardy passage. Questions (a) and (b) have been merged into this opening discussion, which, as already suggested in the examiner's tip, is fine. Here the candidate does manage to cover the first question, about the drama in the writing, in detail, and is going to return to the response of the characters later. A full range of stylistic points is brought out, and he has analysed well the personification and imagery, as well as the sound patterns in the diction. The discussion of the symbolism was also successful. The examiner would be impressed with the way that the symbolism was seen to link various elements of the text.

Hardy's dramatic prose differs vastly in that his style of language involves long, stylish phrases which focus more on the feelings of the characters, especially that of Tess. This exploration of the character's feelings contrasts with Lawrence's attempts to build up the emotion through his striking diction. The dramatic essence of this passage becomes evident towards the end of the extract, when Tess realises what the death of Prince will mean to her family. The actual description of the horse's death, if sad, is not very shocking: 'he suddenly sank down in a heap', and Hardy then goes on to describe the pool of blood from which 'rose a hundred prismatic hues'. This sort of beautiful poetic description brings pathos to the scene and contrasts sharply with Lawrence's whirlwind of violent prose.

Examiner's comment

It is helpful, as the candidate has managed to do here, to consider the alternative passage, whilst at the same time, start to draw out the comparisons.

Because Hardy concentrates so much on emotions, he is very successful at relating the feelings of the characters involved to the events happening around them. The frequent references to Tess herself, described in an emotional condition: 'in consternation', 'despair', 'helplessly looking on', show how upset she is and that she cannot believe the 'dreadful truth'.

Examiner's comment

It is always useful to be make detailed references, as the candidate does in this paragraph. Close reference is such an important skill at this level. The abilities to make comparisons and to use close reference continue well at the start of the next paragraph.

Whereas Lawrence's style involved a kind of violence of emotion and feeling, Hardy's uses violence in another way, almost like a gruesome sort of macabre approach, which is even stronger for being matter of fact:

> 'In her despair Tess sprang forward and put her hand upon the hole, with the only result that she became splashed from face to skirt with the crimson drops.'

Later, she is forced to realise the awful truth of her position in another gruesome moment when she looks rather sadly on at the horse lying dead before her:

> 'Prince lay alongside still and stark; his eyes half open, the hole in his chest looking scarcely large enough to have let out all that had animated him.'

The feelings of the mail-cart man are also seen through his apparent indifference to the situation, which forms a contrast to Tess's plight. He is not in a desperate position, as Tess is, and consequently he is far less emotionally involved. He is more concerned with the delivery of the mail-bags than he is with helping Tess, and he keeps the conversation brief so that he can quickly take his leave and get on with his work.

Lawrence deals less with the emotions of his characters and focuses more on creating the frightening atmosphere brought about by the train. The most descriptive account of a character is of Gudrun reacting to the man riding the horse, because of whom she has 'spellbound eyes' and is 'faint with poignant dizziness'. Ursula's response to the scene is evident from the first line when she cries 'The fool!' but this is all that we learn about her, at least in this extract. The horse-rider has a face 'shining with fixed amusement' but again, this is the only reaction of his that is mentioned. The building up of suspense and fear seem to be paramount in Lawrence's style of writing.

Examiner's comment

We would wish to be slightly critical here, and suggest that the candidate has not really done justice to the way that Lawrence expresses feelings and responses in his characters. We suspect that the candidate has made a common error: in seeking to make a comparison and state a preference for one passage over the other, he may have unnecessarily been too hard on Lawrence and failed to realise that just because his writing is different to Hardy's style, it was no less of merit. True, Lawrence does not explore the inner thoughts and minds of his characters with the same fulsome narrative style that Hardy uses. However, the candidate is rather dismissive of Lawrence's capacity to capture the momentary passions of his characters, especially as the women respond to the violence in the symbolism of the locomotive and horse. The main point to remember is that a comparison does not have to lead you to condemning one extract. The strengths of both can be considered, and arguments found as to why you prefer one. But a preference for one does not imply a distaste for the other.

I believe that Hardy's account is more dramatically effective. Although the passage from *Women in Love* is dramatic, especially in the description of action, Hardy's narrative style has more subtlety, especially in exploring the dramatic nature of the situation through the character. There is more of a build up of the tension and drama in his writing. The reader has to wait for the climax of Tess's hysteria, which is more effective than everything happening at once, as happens in Lawrence's more direct and stronger style. In Hardy's passage, the reader is given more chance to sympathise with the character. It is touching to see how Tess holds herself together, until she responds to the beauty of the morning and how the pool of blood is reflected in the light, her feelings mirrored by the horse, Prince, who:

> 'stood firm and motionless as long as he could'

Both passages involve the characters reacting to the scene around them, but I find the connections in Hardy to be more reflective and expressive of Tess's sad problem. There is a sense of isolation, sadness and pathos in the description of nature waking around the luckless Tess, and yet nature wakes in a way that she cannot, at least not with any human hope in her heart:

> 'The atmosphere turned pale, the birds shook themselves in the hedges, arose, and twittered'

Examiner's comment

Good use of the sense of place, connecting it with character.

I think that the scene is dramatic because neither of them can withstand the pressure they find themselves under, and with Tess this is extreme emotional pressure. This is more effective than the immediate terror of the train in Lawrence's work.

Examiner's comment

The conclusion is mostly relevant: certainly the examiner would be impressed that the candidate is here dealing with character as a way of expressing a preference.

E   APPRECIATION OF A SINGLE EXTRACT OF PROSE

Write an appreciation of the following extract of prose, taken from Joseph Conrad's novel *Lord Jim* (1900). Show how the writing expresses important themes and ideas. What do you imagine has happened and how do you think the events of the passage fit into the novel as a whole?

Lord Jim

EXTRACT

'He heard me out with his head on one side, and I had another glimpse through a rent in the mist in which he moved and had his being. The dim candle spluttered within the ball of glass, and that was all I had to see him by; at his back was the dark night with the clear stars, whose distant glitter disposed in retreating planes lured the eye into the depths of a greater darkness; and yet a mysterious light seemed to show me his boyish head, as if in that moment the youth within him had, for a moment, gleamed and expired. "You are an awful good sort to listen like this," he said. "It does me good. You don't know what it is to me. You don't . . ." words seemed to fail him. It was a distinct glimpse. He was a youngster of the sort you like to see about you; of the sort whose appearance claims the fellowship of these illusions you had thought gone out, extinct, cold, and which, as if rekindled at the approach of another flame, give a flutter deep, deep down somewhere, give a flutter of light . . . of heat! . . . Yes; I had a glimpse of him then . . . and it was not the last of that kind . . . . "You don't know what it is for a fellow in my position to be believed — make a clean breast of it to an elder man. It is so difficult — so awfully unfair — so hard to understand."

'The mists were closing again. I don't know how old I appeared to him — and how much wise. Not half as old as I felt just then; not half as uselessly wise as I knew myself to be. Surely in no other craft as in that of the sea do the hearts of those already launched to sink or swim go out so much to the youth on the brink, looking with shining eyes upon that glitter of the vast surface which is only a reflection of his own glances full of fire. There is such magnificent vagueness in the expectations that had driven each of us to sea, such glorious indefiniteness, such a beautiful greed of adventures that are their own and only reward! What we get — well, we won't talk of that; but can one of us restrain a smile? In no other kind of life is the illusion more wide of reality — in no other is the beginning *all* illusion — the disenchantment more swift — the subjugation more complete. Hadn't we all commenced with the same desire, ended with the same knowledge, carried the memory of the same cherished glamour through the sordid days of imprecation? What wonder that when some heavy prod gets home the bond is found to be close; that besides the fellowship of the craft there is felt the strength of a wider feeling — the feeling that binds a man to a child. He was there before me, believing that age and wisdom can find a remedy against the pain of truth, giving me a glimpse of himself as a young fellow in a scrape that is the very devil of a scrape, the sort of scrape greybeards wag at solemnly while they hide a smile. And he had been deliberating upon death — confound him! He had found *that* to meditate about because he thought he had saved his life, while all its glamour had gone with the ship in the night. What more natural! It was tragic enough and funny enough in all conscience to call aloud for compassion, and in what was I better than the rest of us to refuse him my pity? And even as I looked at him the mists rolled into the tent, and his voice spoke —

' "I was so lost, you know. It was the sort of thing one does not expect to happen to one. It was not like a fight, for instance."

' "It was not," I admitted. He appeared changed, as if he had suddenly matured.

' "One couldn't be sure," he muttered.

' "Ah! You were not sure," I said, and was placated by the sound of a faint sigh that passed between us like the flight of a bird in the night.'

JOSEPH CONRAD

Examiner's tip

Before you start this answer, make sure that you have identified, through the key words in the instructions, exactly what you are being asked to focus on. You are asked firstly to concentrate on **themes** and **ideas**. The passage is a powerful one, structured partly on a conversation between an older and a younger sailor, and partly on the inner thoughts of the older man. You would need to show how both these features: the conversation and the private thinking, bring out themes and meanings. You need also to note that you are asked to deal with **important** themes and meanings. The examiner will be looking to assess how well you have understood major issues about human experience.

The last part of the question is unusual, but when you think about it, it is similar to those types of question which ask you for a personal response. Just as you can be asked to state how the opening to a novel can entice you to read on, here you are being asked to predict or speculate from the context not of an opening passage, but of a central extract. Make sure your material is relevant, and above all, provide evidence for any speculations you make, directly from the passage.

Important themes and ideas concerning the ways in which people understand their past experiences of life are brought out in this passage by Joseph Conrad. As well as this, there is an overlap of themes which all have to do with hope, doubt and destiny. It is my opinion that these are important themes and ideas because they are the sort of points which encourage the reader to think about the meaning of life, about how things can go wrong and about how we can live with ourselves in the full knowledge that things go wrong and that mistakes are there to haunt us, no matter how old we get to be.

ANSWER

Examiner's comment

A helpful and confident introduction, showing immediate confidence and security with the requirements of the question. It is particularly good to see comments on the relationship between the reader and writer. This will impress the examiner as it is a key skill, and will now, we hope, be developed.

Before discussing the themes, it is helpful to show what is happening, as this provides a context for such a deep and meaningful level of discussion as takes place between the two characters. It would seem that the younger character, a sea-going man but one less experienced than the narrator, has undergone a terrifying or distressing event whilst working at sea. He is described as 'a young fellow in a scrape' and furthermore, we know it was dramatic because it was 'the very devil of a scrape'. The young man knows exactly what happened to him, but the main clue is when the older character, who acts as a kind of listener, says:

> 'he thought he had saved his life, while all its glamour had gone with the ship in the night.'

The suggestion hinted at is that the young man's ship has been in an accident and he has survived it, only to live like a kind of haunted ghost with the horror of the vessel going down and the guilt that he has survived. There is irony in the phrase 'he thought he had saved his life,' because of the kind of living death that he has had to suffer through his trial of self-doubt and eternal guilt.

Whatever it was that did actually occur, the reader also knows that this young man was facing a difficult situation, one in which it was not easy for him to make decisions:

> 'I was so lost, you know. It was the sort of thing one does not expect to happen to one.'

I think there is evidence to show that in the remainder of the novel he, the young sailor, will be trying to rediscover the past in order to come to terms with himself. The evidence for this comes when he says: 'One couldn't be sure' and as we know that he may have 'suddenly matured', he may be about to try to resolve the nagging self-doubt in order to purge it from his life. He may not, however, manage to do this and so another possibility is that he will sink further into depression and perhaps eventually commit suicide; in this way the maturity will have led to punishment and penance.

Examiner's comment

It does not matter that the candidate has answered the last part of the question here nearer the beginning of the answer. It is a sensible option and has been handled well. The ideas about the relationship between this passage and the events in the novel as a whole are argued in detail and — this is particularly good — are linked closely as possibilities to the evidence in the text, through impressive referencing.

In the passage itself the events of the past clearly have a bearing on the mood of the present and there is also an important part to be played by the older character. In fact, it is his interpretation of what he hears that brings out more forcefully the most powerful themes.

He reflects on the passing of youth as he picks out the young man's face by the spluttering light of the dim candle against the greater darkness of night behind him. This is perhaps a symbol of the extinguishing of youth, giving way to the gloom of experience. However, the confrontation with the young man, with the sensitive play of light on his face from the candle, has something important to say to the narrator about the pain involved in the passing of life, this distancing of youth. This gave 'a flutter' - rekindling 'these illusions you had thought gone out.'

The writer further develops his themes through the build up of the relationship between the two characters. As the mists close in, as if symbolically obscuring ideas, the older sailor, acting as a priest might do as a confessor, comes to hold his own feelings of self-doubt and uncertainty, particularly about the value of age and wisdom.

There are ideas of destiny, false expectation and destroyed hope expressed as the older man thinks about what he calls the 'glorious indefiniteness' in the adventures of a sea-faring life, and although the younger man may on the surface have more need to pour out his heart, it is the older who suffers more through these trials of 'deliberating upon death':

> 'Hadn't we all commenced with the same desire, ended with the same knowledge, carried the memory of the same cherished glamour through the sordid days of imprecation?'

Conrad uses this recollection of an awful event and the listening heart of the older character who in the end comes to pity his younger friend, to express many questions: What is it like to live with your past? How do we live with the let-down of experience? These are perhaps the two most powerful questions, and the interesting feature of the form of the writing is that they come to be more important for the older man, who acts as a link with the reader, rather than the younger.

Examiner's comment

An excellent, stylish essay. All the criteria for the highest marks are fully met: the question is answered very thoroughly with detailed analysis supported by close reference. It is also refreshing for an examiner to come across a candidate who can refer so naturally to the importance of symbolism (the mist and the candle) and to the form and structure (the nature of the conversation).

In the appreciations you write about extracts of drama, you will particularly need to:

- show how the dialogue works to create character and theme;
- be aware of the fact that drama is meant for the theatre;
- comment on any additional features, such as stage directions, which contribute to the overall purpose of the work;
- bring out meanings and ideas which are conveyed through speeches, and point to the elegance and beauty of this language where appropriate;
- recognise dramatic climaxes, anti-climaxes, and other shifts in mood;
- comment when necessary on the settings of dramatic extracts;
- show what form or genre of drama is being used: realistic, mythical, historical, ritualistic, comic, tragic etc.;
- show why characters sometimes speak in verse, and how rhetorical devices have a part to play in certain works.

A STUDYING AN EXTRACT OF JACOBEAN DRAMA

In the play *Volpone* by Ben Jonson (1616), the central character, Volpone, spends much of the time pretending to be bedridden as he finds this suits his purpose. In this, Act 3 of the play, his lusting after the innocent Celia causes him to drop his defences.

Analyse how, in this scene, Ben Jonson controls the situation by examining his use of language and imagery. You should also consider his use of song and theatrical device.

Volpone

EXTRACT

VOLPONE: Why are thou mazed, to see me thus revived?
Rather applaud thy beauty's miracle;
'Tis thy great work, that hath, not now alone,
But sundry times raised me in several shapes,
And, but this morning, like a mountebank,
To see thee at thy window. Ay, before
I would have left my practice for thy love,
In varying figures, I would have contended
With blue Proteus, or the hornèd flood.
Now, art thou welcome.

CELIA: Sir!

VOLPONE: Nay, fly me not,
Nor let thy false imagination
That I was bed-rid, make thee think I am so:
Thou shalt not find it. I am, now, as fresh,
As hot, as high, and in as jovial plight
As when, in that so celebrated scene,
At recitation of our comedy,
For entertainment of the young Valois,
I acted young Antinous, and attracted
The eyes and ears of all the ladies present,
T'admire each graceful gesture, note and footing.

SONG

Come, my Celia, let us prove,
While we can, the sports of love;
Time will not be ours forever,
He, at length, our good will sever;
Spend not then his gifts in vain.
Suns that set may rise again;
But if once we lose this light,
'Tis with us perpetual night.
Why should we defer our joys?
Fame and rumour are but toys.
Cannot we delude the eyes
Of a few poor household spies?
Or his easier ears beguile,
Thus removèd by our wile?
'Tis no sin love's fruits to steal,
But the sweet thefts to reveal:
To be taken, to be seen,
These have crimes accounted been.

CELIA: Some *serene* blast me, or dire lightning strike
This my offending face.

VOLPONE: Why droops my Celia?
Thou hast in place of a base husband found
A worthy lover; use thy fortune well,
With secrecy and pleasure. See, behold,
What thou art queen of;
Not in expectation,
As I feed others, but possessed and crowned.
See, here, a rope of pearl, and each more orient
Than the brave Egyptian queen caroused;
Dissolve and drink 'em. See, a carbuncle
May put out both the eyes of our St Mark;
A diamond would have bought Lollia Paulina
When she came in, like star-light, hid with jewels
That were the spoils of provinces; take these,
And wear, and lose 'em; yet remains an ear-ring
To purchase them again, and this whole state.
A gem but worth a private patrimony
Is nothing: we will eat such at a meal.
The heads of parrots, tongues of nightingales,
The brains of peacocks, and of ostriches
Shall be our food, and, could we get the phoenix,
Though nature lost her kind, she were our dish.

CELIA: Good sir, these things might move a mind affected
With such delights; but I, whose innocence
Is all I can think wealthy, or worth th' enjoying
And which, once lost, I have nought to lose beyond it,
Cannot be taken with these sensual baits.
If you have conscience —

VOLPONE: 'Tis the beggar's virtue.
If thou hast wisdom, hear me, Celia.
Thy baths shall be the juice of July-flowers,

Spirits of roses, and of violets,
The milk of unicorns, and panthers' breath
Gathered in bags and mixed with Cretan wines.
Our drink shall be preparèd gold, and amber,
Which we will take until my roof whirl round
With the vertigo; and my dwarf shall dance,
My eunuch sing, my fool make up the antic.
Whilst we, in changèd shapes, act Ovid's tales,
Thou like Europa now, and I like Jove,
Then I like Mars, and thou like Erycine;
So of the rest of us, till we have quite run through,
And wearied all the fables of the gods.
Then will I have thee in more modern forms,
Attirèd like some sprightly dame of France,
Brave Tuscan lady, or proud Spanish beauty;
Sometimes unto the Persian Sophy's wife,
Or the Grand Signor's mistress; and, for a change,
To one of our most artful courtesans,
Or some quick Negro, or cold Russian;
And I will meet thee in as many shapes;
Where we may so transfuse our wand'ring souls
Out at our lips and score up sums of pleasures, (*Sings*)
That the curious shall not know
How to tell them as they flow;
And the envious, when they find
What their number is, be pined.

CELIA: If you have ears that will be pierced, or eyes
That can be opened, a heart may be touched,
Or any part that yet sounds man about you;
If you have touch of holy saints, or heaven,
Do me the grace to let me 'scape. If not,
Be bountiful and kill me. You do know
I am a creature hither ill betrayed
By one whose shame I would forget it were.
If you will deign me neither of these graces,
Yet feed your wrath, sir, rather than your lust,
(It is a vice, comes nearer manliness)
And punish that unhappy crime of nature,
Which you miscall my beauty; flay my face,
Or poison it with ointments for seducing
Your blood to this rebellion. Rub these hands
With what may cause an eating leprosy,
E'en to my bones and marrow; anything
That may disfavour me, save in my honour,
And I will kneel to you, pray for you, pay down
A thousand hourly vows, sir, for your health;
Report, and think you virtuous —

VOLPONE: Think me cold,
Frozen, and impotent, and so report me?
That I had Nestor's hernia, thou wouldst think.
I do degenerate and abuse my nation
To play with opportunity this long;
I should have done the act, and then have parleyed.

	Yield, or I'll force thee.
CELIA:	O! just God!
VOLPONE:	In vain —
BONARIO:	Forbear, foul ravisher! libidinous swine!

He leaps out from where MOSCA *had placed him.*

Free the forced lady, or thou diest, impostor.
But that I am loath to snatch thy punishment
Out of the hand of justice, thou shouldst yet
Be made the timely sacrifice of vengeance,
Before this altar, and this dross, thy idol.
Lady, let's quit this place, it is the den
Of villainy; fear nought, you have a guard;
And he ere long shall meet his just reward.

[Exeunt BONARIO *and* CELIA.*]*

VOLPONE:	Fall on me, roof, and bury me in ruin!
	Become my grave, that wert my shelter! O!
	I am unmasked, unspirited, undone,
	Betrayed to beggary, to infamy —

[Enter MOSCA, *wounded and bleeding.]*

MOSCA:	Where shall I run, most wretched shame of men,
	To beat out my unlucky brains?
VOLPONE:	Here, here.
	What, dost thou bleed?
MOSCA:	O, that his well-driven sword
	Had been so courteous to have cleft me down
	Unto the navel, ere I lived to see
	My life, my hopes, my spirits, my patron, all
	Thus desperately engagèd, by my error.
VOLPONE:	Woe on thy fortune!
MOSCA:	And my follies, sir.
VOLPONE:	Th' hast made me miserable.
MOSCA:	And myself, sir.
	Who would have thought he would have hearkened so?
VOLPONE:	What shall we do?

BEN JONSON

---

and also to his considerable worldliness. It is a good idea to say something about the melodramatic tone of his speech, and to bring this out with references to the voluptuous and inspiring imagery as well as the logical argument that he sometimes engages.

The song allows him to present himself in the position of a courtier, with the use of seductive and clever argument. This is a technique which allows Volpone to express his lust for Celia.

The central character in this scene, Volpone, cleverly manipulates the situation throughout by appealing to Celia with a variety of techniques of flattery and exaggeration. He begins this sort of flattery by asking her a direct question which is meant to put her in a position where she recognises that his recovery is due to her beauty:

> 'Rather applaud thy beauty's miracle'

This is designed to make her feel important and to stress her beauty. It is the first of many examples of sheer seductiveness. In this first section, he continues to make her feel important by trying to surprise her. He tells her that he would have left his practice for her love earlier. Her short response in the simple word 'Sir!' reveals that he has the desired effect; he has managed to control her emotions and she is immediately in a state of shock. This opening gambit in the seduction has been designed to make Celia feel immensely important.

Following this, in his second speech, Volpone shows a great deal of energy. His statements are very direct and so Celia is left in no doubt as to the vitality he possesses towards her. This particularly comes across in the lines:

> '. . . I am, now, as fresh,
> As hot, as high, and in as jovial plight . . .'

This degree of honesty leads him to compare his present situation to the time when he 'acted young Antinous', which lends him an opportunity to present himself not just in a theatrical light, but one in which he gained the admiration of 'all the ladies present'.

As this gives rise to his song, we discover that what Volpone is doing is presenting conscious seductive arguments. He certainly knows precisely what he is doing, and he comes across as a character very much in control of his situation. In the song the challenge he sets Celia is to 'prove . . . the sports of love' and his reasons for this are all connected with a disturbing but persuasive theme of time. Time is personified in the song, and time will destroy them if they do not take advantage of their opportunity now. Indeed, if they do not do so:

> ''Tis with us perpetual night.'

The fact that he uses song for this argument, which also deals with moral themes of sin and virtue — really he seems to be making a virtue out of the idea of their liaison — means that his appeal is more direct and assertive. The effect on Celia is not, however, successful:

> 'Some serene blast me, or dire lightning strike
> This my offending face.'

Volpone seems incapable of being rebuffed by her rejections. In fact, the more he is rejected by Celia, the more he appears to discover the energy to continue and to find additional arguments. Each argument and technique of seduction steps up the pressure on her, and further expresses his relentless determination. In his speech beginning: ' Why droops my Celia?', he uses a number of contrasts characterised in the style by breaks in the lines to make her feel not just an important and irresistible woman, but also to entice her through

sensual experience in his bribery. This kind of seduction places her in a position of being a kind of queen, and as such she can enjoy all that he is offering her. She is offered jewels, feasts and riches in a stunning display of apparent generosity designed to make her the most important and well-endowed lover in the world. Volpone uses language here to mesmerise her in the pursuit of his prize. It is a glittering display of delights, but they do not 'move' her as she is not of a mind to give in to him.

I believe that what Volpone is doing is engaging in a kind of courtly seduction which is meant to suggest the idea of a feast ending in the sexual act. The feast outlined at the end of the speech ends with the hyperbole which hints at his climactic desires:

> '. . . could we get the phoenix,
> Though nature lost her kind, she were our dish.'

At this point, he is, however, no further advanced in his plan, as she still rejects him, and she does so in a way which reveals that she is well aware what he is doing. She retorts that her 'innocence is all I can think wealthy'. So his renewed energy takes him into the ploy of comparisons through nature imagery and classical allusion. He tries to entice her through a sensual reference to nature, and shows himself to be a master of fine rhetorical language and poetic effect as he does so, one example being the alliteration in the powerful line:

> 'Thy baths shall be the juice of July-flowers'

As if this sensual world of nature is not sufficient for her potential pleasure, his further appeal is to the gods. She will be placed in a world which will become more than human, and will enjoy her pleasure with him as the gods themselves did:

> 'Thou like Europa now, and I like Jove,
> Then I like Mars, and thou like Erycine'

This is a very strong appeal, and is part of a repertoire of seductive techniques which show that Volpone is fully in command of all aspects of the world. By this, I mean that he can successfully switch from reference to classical elements, to nature and to the real world. Indeed, he passes from the imagery of the gods to the new world, and we begin to feel that he is truly a man of the world, conscious of the expanding Renaissance society. He will move about from one shape to another and represent himself to her in many different forms:

> '. . . some quick Negro, or cold Russian;
> And I will meet thee in as many shapes'

This is a final exotic appeal and is designed to present him in the light of a complete lover, one who has many talents and is capable of taking on many roles in life.

There may, however, be something acutely ironic about all this exaggeration, as we are going to learn at the end of the scene that all his attempts are in vain. This seems to lend an added purpose to the exaggerated style of some of his exotic language, as he is perhaps carried away by his own convictions, and cannot see the foolishness of what he is doing, in spite of the way that Celia rejects him on every occasion. Perhaps the exaggeration in his style is even encouraged by his being in a state of lust.

Volpone does feel he is in control, and this confidence is expressed through techniques of language that are immensely varied. A few examples are: his capacity to exaggerate and to use hyperbole, intended to make Celia feel an important and desired woman: 'thy beauty's miracle'; 'behold, What thou art queen of'. He can vary his tone so that one moment he may be speaking in terms of poetic rhetoric, and then the next he speaks directly, in a highly personal and commanding manner: 'Nay, fly me not'. He is a master of exotic imagery. In particular from the line: ''Tis the beggar's virtue' onwards he creates a colourful scene through the imagery of nature, animals, food and drink, which is full of great wealth and

delight. It is succulent and physical, deliberately meant to be sensual, as part of the process of seduction:

> 'The milk of unicorns, and panthers' breath
> Gathered in bags and mixed with Cretan wines.'

He shows himself to be very knowledgeable of the world, its history and its new geography, as well as its classical past and its wealthy possessions. He uses all this knowledge to dramatise pictures and scenes in a very active way, presumably in order to command Celia's wavering and doubting attention:

> '. . . take these,
> And wear, and lose 'em; yet remains an ear-ring
> To purchase them again'

Finally, like a Metaphysical Poet, he manages to offer strong arguments built around powerful themes such as the need to conquer time: 'To play with opportunity this long', transfiguration: 'Where we may so transfuse our wand'ring souls' and fortune. These seem very much part of the world of the start of the seventeenth century, when the play was written — a world of new wonders and openings, with the importation of new riches from distant lands.

Examiner's comment

This candidate has made a lot of sense of the extract, and finds a way through to understanding the rhetoric used by the central character. The answer reveals well how there is a variety of techniques in use, through argument, imagery and flattery, and these are organised in a clear and logical way. The candidate also has a sense of the new world in which Jonson was writing, so that, although there is not a great deal of comment on the historical context, there is at least recognition that the work is Jacobean.

It has been a good idea for the candidate to move steadily through the extract, as this has lead to a painstaking and full analysis.

B ANALYSING CHARACTERISATION IN DRAMA

In this passage, an extract from *The Widowing of Mrs Holroyd*, by D H Lawrence (1933) the scene is set in a miner's cottage. An accident in the pit has killed Holroyd, and here we see his body being brought home to his wife and mother (the character known as Grandmother). Mr Blackmore is also in attendance.

In your analysis of the scene, show how successful Lawrence is at creating the pathos of the situation, and consider the ways that he brings out the different reactions of the characters to the tragedy. Also, attempt to show how he manages to document the tragic lives of this mining community.

The Widowing of Mrs Holroyd

EXTRACT

> *There is a quick sound of footsteps.* BLACKMORE *comes into the light of the doorway.*
>
> BLACKMORE: They're bringing him.
> MRS HOLROYD (*quickly putting her hand to her breast*): What is it?
> BLACKMORE: You can't tell anything's the matter with him — he's not marked at all.

MRS HOLROYD: Oh, what a blessing! And is it much?

BLACKMORE: Well —

MRS HOLROYD: What is it?

BLACKMORE: It's the worst.

GRANDMOTHER: Who is it?— What does he say?

> MRS HOLROYD *sinks on the nearest chair with a horrified expression.* BLACKMORE *pulls himself together and enters the room. He is very pale.*

BLACKMORE: I came to tell you they're bringing him home.

GRANDMOTHER: And you said it wasn't very bad, did you?

BLACKMORE: No — I said it was — as bad as could be.

MRS HOLROYD (*rising and crossing to her mother-in-law, flings her arms around her; in a high voice*): Oh, mother, what shall we do? What shall we do?

GRANDMOTHER: You don't mean to say he's dead?

BLACKMORE: Yes.

GRANDMOTHER (*staring*): God help us, and how was it?

BLACKMORE: Some stuff fell.

GRANDMOTHER (*rocking herself and her daughter-in-law — both weeping*): Oh, God have mercy on us! Oh, God have mercy on us! Some stuff fell on him. An' he'd not even time to cry for mercy; oh, God spare him! Oh, what shall we do for comfort? To be taken straight out of his sins. Oh, Lizzie, to think he should be cut off in his wickedness. He's been a bad lad of late, he has, poor lamb. He's gone very wrong of late years, poor lamb, very wrong. Oh, Lizzie, think what's become of him now! If you'd only tried to be different with him.

MRS HOLROYD (*moaning*): Don't, mother, don't. I can't bear it.

BLACKMORE (*cold and clear*): Where will you have him laid? The men will be here in a moment.

MRS HOLROYD (*staring up*): They can carry him up to bed —

BLACKMORE: It's no good taking him upstairs. You'll have to wash him and lay him out.

MRS HOLROYD (*startled*): Well —

BLACKMORE: He's in his pit-dirt.

GRANDMOTHER: He is, bless him. We'd better have him down here, Lizzie, where we can handle him.

MRS HOLROYD: Yes.

> She begins to put the tea things away, but drops the sugar out of the basin and the lumps fly broadcast.

BLACKMORE: Never mind, I'll pick those up. You put the children's clothes away.

> MRS HOLROYD *stares witless around. The* GRANDMOTHER *sits rocking herself and weeping.* BLACKMORE *clears the table, putting the pots in the scullery. He folds the white tablecloth and pulls back the table. The door opens,* MRS HOLROYD *utters a cry.* RIGLEY *enters.*

RIGLEY: They're bringing him now, missus.

MRS HOLROYD: Oh!

RIGLEY (*simply*): There must ha' been a fall directly after we left him.

MRS HOLROYD (*frowning, horrified*): No — no!

RIGLEY (*to* BLACKMORE): It fell a' back of him, an' shut 'im in as you might shut a loaf i' th' oven. It never touched him.

MRS HOLROYD (*staring distractedly*): Well, then —

RIGLEY: You see, it come on 'im as close as a trap on a mouse, an' gen him no air, an' what wi' th' gas, it smothered him. An' it wouldna be so very long about it neither.

MRS HOLROYD (*quiet with horror*): Oh!

GRANDMOTHER: Eh, dear — dear. Eh, dear — dear.

RIGLEY (*looking hard at her*): I wasna to know what 'ud happen.

GRANDMOTHER (*not heeding him, but weeping all the time*): But the Lord gave him time to repent. He'd have a few minutes to repent. Ay, I hope he did, I hope he did, else what was to become of him? The Lord cut him off in his sins, but He gave him time to repent.

> RIGLEY *looks away at the wall.* BLACKMORE *has made a space in the middle of the floor.*

BLACKMORE: If you'll take the rocking-chair off the end of the rug, Mrs Holroyd, I can pull it back a bit from the fire, and we can lay him on that.

GRANDMOTHER(*petulantly*): What's the good of messing about — (*She moves.*)

MRS HOLROYD: It suffocated him?

RIGLEY (*shaking his head, briefly*): Yes. 'Appened th' after-damp —

BLACKMORE: He'd be dead in a few minutes.

MRS HOLROYD: No — oh, think!

BLACKMORE: You mustn't think.

RIGLEY (*suddenly*): They commin'!

> MRS HOLROYD *stands at bay. The* GRANDMOTHER *half rises.* RIGLEY *and* BLACKMORE *efface themselves as much as possible. A man backs into the room, bearing the feet of the dead man, which are shod in great pit boots. As the head bearer comes awkwardly past the table, the coat with which the body is covered slips off, revealing* HOLROYD *in his pit-dirt, naked to the waist.*

D H LAWRENCE

Examiner's tip

This is a very naturalistic work of drama, and the examiner will consequently be looking to see how well you manage to bring out the dramatic tension of the scene from language which is, by its nature, rather ordinary. Lawrence has represented real people in a tragic situation, and the key to the feelings expressed lies in the way that there is terrible grief and pathos set alongside the dialect of ordinary working people who have to perform mundane tasks, such as the putting away of the children's clothes, before the body is brought in. There is also great suffering depicted in a style which, to some extent, documents the hard and fatalistic lives of the mining community. The best answers will draw on the interactions between each character, as well as the preoccupations expressed through their language, and the stage directions which quite explicitly set a deliberately natural domestic scene.

ANSWER

This extract begins with Blackmore's rather ironic statement 'You can't tell anything's the matter with him', which conceals the awful truth about Holroyd's death. In my opinion, this attitude is there in the text in order to show that Blackmore finds it very difficult to speak the truth about the man's death in front of the wife and grandmother. In this first exchange of conversation between Blackmore and Mrs Holroyd, we sense from her mixed emotions, when first of all she appears to enjoy great relief that he is 'not marked' and then terrible anguish as she sinks on the nearest chair with a horrified expression that she has in fact been waiting to hear the worst. This may be partly why she is able to cope with the situation later in the scene, at least with greater dignity and bearing than the grandmother. Blackmore obviously has to be respectful and this leads him to understate the news in a nervous and troubled way.

One of the features of the text that I find immediately interesting is the way that the mother and grandmother react so differently to the news. They are both rocking and weeping, but the grandmother's grief is more prominent and more openly expressed, in the speech which begins: 'Oh, God have mercy on us!' By concentrating his attention on this exchange between mother and daughter-in-law, Lawrence manages to focus on the characters, and especially on the quiet but intense grief that we come to see so strongly as part of Mrs Holroyd's character. In a sense she becomes the central character as the strongest point of focus is on her. This is not just because she is the widow, but because of the dignified anguish that she is suffering.

Once the initial shock is over there is a practical theme which is established, to do with the fact that life must go on, and decisions have to be made. It seems so inopportune a moment to have to make a decision about where to lay the body, but this little negotiation is necessary because he is still 'in his pit-dirt' and so cannot be taken upstairs to bed. This awkward conversation, along with the fact that the tea things and the children's clothes will have to be put away, adds to the extreme naturalness of the scene and stresses the fact that these are the lives of real people, so the tragedy is one which documents what must have happened in the lives of many miners from time to time. They are poor people, obviously, and such basic practical decisions about where to lay out the body, have to be made. Yet as these practical activities are taking centre stage, there is a contrast with the awful grief felt by Mrs Holroyd, symbolised particularly by the way that she *drops the sugar out of the basin and the lumps fly broadcast.*

Through these sorts of symbols of her distracted grief, she shows her reactions, all the time the grandmother is openly expressing her feelings: *The Grandmother sits rocking herself and weeping.* And Blackmore is also characterised as a man who feels understandably uncomfortable, as if he is intruding in an affair of great private grief. He busies himself, surely to some extent taking charge of the situation, by clearing away the pots in the scullery and by folding the white tablecloth and pulling back the table.

Rigley is then introduced into the scene, and his language has a lot to contribute to its sad themes. The interesting thing is that he speaks in a deadpan kind of way, with the truth bluntly revealed, and sadly this draws attention to what must have actually happened in the accident:

> Rigley (*simply*): There must ha' been a fall directly after we left him.

This dimension of the added realism of the accident and the death contributes a sense of shock as the full horror of his likely suffocation begins to become clear. It is also probable that Lawrence wants the audience to understand, through an awareness of Holroyd's death, just how vulnerable the miners were in their work, and so there are themes of suffering and fate which are introduced.

Again, we get very different reactions to this news from the characters, just as we did earlier in the scene when there were initial reactions to the news. Mrs Holroyd seems to withdraw into herself as she becomes aware of the anguish that her husband must have felt at the moment of his death, when he had very little time to fight his way out of the problem: (*quiet with horror*) 'Oh!' The grandmother is reduced to a kind of hysteria which becomes uncontrollable and which begins to centre on her fears for her son's salvation. It may be that Lawrence is being quite critical of her attitude when he presents her outburst about Holroyd's repentance:

> 'The Lord cut him off in his sins, but He gave him time to repent.'

The possibility of a critical attitude is there because she contrasts so sharply again with the calmness of Mrs Holroyd, who is suffering inside herself, but does not need to wail and weep in quite such an ostentatious manner. Mrs Holroyd does reveal, however, that even though her grief is quiet and private, she is contemplating the events as they might have happened, and wants to know the details of what happened:

> 'It suffocated him?'

Blackmore continues his helpful role with wise counsel that she would do better not to try and think about what happened. I find this quite moving. It is an exchange which again draws attention to the conflict between life and death, which is a theme that emerges, I find, throughout the focus on the behaviour and character of Mrs Holroyd in this scene. When Blackmore tells her: 'You mustn't think', he reinforces the idea that the living must pay attention to their own affairs, and we sympathise with Mrs Holroyd as one who must get on with the practicalities of death. On the other hand, the words provide us, potentially, with a gruesome picture of the accident, which will stay to haunt Mrs Holroyd long afterwards.

Some of the stage directions have already been mentioned as important, but they become even more so when the body of the dead miner is brought into the house. Lawrence makes sure at this point that all the characters react in a way that expresses each of their reactions. Mrs Holroyd stands at bay signifies the way that she must get on with the job, and does not wish to be in the way as the body is carried in. The fact that the grandmother 'half rises' makes me think that she is in an uncontrollable state of suffering and anguish, and is merely trying to pull herself together now, and the self-effacement of Blackmore and Rigley clearly confirm their polite, respectful attitudes which adds to the dignity and pathos of the incident.

The way that he is brought in, naked to the waist, his feet in pit boots and his body covered in pit dirt, reaffirms the other major theme which Lawrence wants to put across, which is the hardship and sacrifice involved in mining. Here we have a corpse brought into its own front room, while the family life is going on around him (there was earlier mention of children's clothing — presumably they, the children, are asleep upstairs while all this trauma happens). There is nowhere else for the body to be taken, and Mrs Holroyd and her mother-in-law face the prospect now of cleaning the body of pit dirt, which is just one more job that needs to be done, in the nature of things.

Lawrence's style of writing manages to create the pathos, to show the differences in the reactions of the characters, and also helps to depict the suffering of the community of miners. There is a quiet, respectful style of language in all the exchanges between Mrs Holroyd and Blackmore. Lawrence deliberately restrains the speech of Mrs Holroyd, so that she often speaks one word in surprise or shock, as a way of expressing the full horror that must be filling her mind. The style of the grandmother's language is presented as more of an incantation, wailing her grief for all to hear. I am not suggesting that this is necessarily self-indulgent — after all, it would be understandable, but it does offer a contrast with the restraint of her daughter-in-law, and at a time when dignity is required, appears rather clumsy. I suspect that in the way the play might develop, the purpose of her public outcry is to help the audience focus on the way that poor Mrs Holroyd has to get on with things, and I wonder whether there is even some conflict between the two women.

Finally, the bold way that the details of the death and the return of the body are dealt with give an insight into the sacrifice and hardship of the community. Rigley's frank details, presented in a style of almost proverbial matter-of-factness: 'a loaf i' th' oven' or 'a trap on a mouse', the handling of a body which has to be prepared on the table, the clearing away of the clothes, etc. — all this, enhanced by the precise stage directions, lends a natural reality to the scene. Although the tragedy will have been unique for each family to lose a man in the mine, there is a sense in which this is an everyday occurrence, so that when Blackmore says 'It's no good taking him upstairs. You'll have to wash him and lay him out' we realise that he has been in this tragic situation hundreds of times over.

This is an excellent, full answer which is written in a stylish and often elegant manner. The candidate does precisely what is asked, detailing the different reactions of the characters by using close examples of their speech, from the text. In particular we were impressed by the candidate's understanding of the role of Mrs Holroyd, and the way she expressed her feelings, through restrained dignity. This was argued in a concise and sensitive manner.

There is also fine understanding of the purpose of the realism, and at times there is a well-expressed analysis of the documentary value of the drama, as it shows something about the tragedies and horrors of such a dangerous life.

This candidate reveals awareness that the drama constructs the tragedy, i.e. through the dialogue, the movements and the stage directions.

C STUDYING EMOTIONS IN A DRAMATIC EXTRACT

Read the following extract from *A Man for all Seasons* by Robert Bolt (1960), a modern work of historical drama. The situation is that Sir Thomas More has been imprisoned for refusing to support Henry VIII's actions in establishing himself as the supreme head of the Church in England, following the break with Rome. On this occasion he is receiving a visit in gaol from his family: his wife Alice, daughter Margaret and son-in-law, Will Roper.

Comment in detail on the means by which the dramatist expresses the emotions of the situation and discuss any ideas and themes which are presented during these exchanges between the characters.

EXTRACT

A Man for all Seasons

MARGARET: Good morning, Father.

MORE (*ecstatic, wraps her to him*): Oh, good morning — Good morning. (*Enter* ALICE, *supported by* WILL. *She, like* MORE, *has aged and is poorly dressed.*) Good morning, Alice. Good morning, Will.

ROPER *is staring at the rack in horror.* ALICE *approaches* MORE *and peers at him technically.*

ALICE (*almost accusatory*): Husband, how do you?

MORE (*smiling over at* MARGARET): As well as need be, Alice. Very happy now. Will?

ROPER: This is an awful place!

MORE: Except it's keeping me from you, my dears, it's not so bad. Remarkably like any other place.

ALICE (*looks up critically*): It drips!

MORE: Yes, too near the river. (ALICE *goes apart and sits, her face bitter.*)

MARGARET (*disengages from him, takes basket from her mother*): We've brought you some things. (*Shows him. There is constraint between them.*) Some cheese . . .

MORE: Cheese . . .

MARGARET: And a custard . . .

MORE: A custard!

MARGARET: And, these other things . . . (*She doesn't look at him.*)

ROPER: And a bottle of wine. (*Offering it.*)

MORE: Oh. (*Mischievous.*) Is it good, son Roper?

ROPER: I don't know, sir.

MORE (*looks at them, puzzled*): Well.

ROPER: Sir, come out! Swear to the Act! Take the oath and come out!

MORE: Is this why they let you come?

ROPER: Yes . . . Meg's under oath to persuade you.

MORE (*coldly*): That was silly, Meg. How did you come to that?

MARGARET: I wanted to!

MORE: You want me to swear to the Act of Succession?

MARGARET: 'God more regards the thoughts of the heart than the words of the mouth' or so you've always told me.

MORE: Yes.

MARGARET: Then say the words of the oath and in your heart think otherwise.

MORE: What is an oath then but words we say to God?

MARGARET: That's very neat.

MORE: Then it's a poor argument to call it 'neat', Meg. When a man takes an oath, Meg, he's holding his own self in his own hands. Like water (*cups hands*) and if he opens his fingers then — he needn't hope to find himself again. Some men aren't capable of this, but I'd be loath to think your father one of them.

MARGARET: So should I . . .

MORE: Then —

MARGARET: There's something else I've been thinking.

MORE: Oh, Meg!

MARGARET: In any state that was half good, you would be raised up high, not here, for what you've done already.

MORE: All right.

MARGARET: It's not your fault the state's three-quarters bad.

MORE: No.

MARGARET: Then if you elect to suffer for it, you elect yourself a hero.

MORE: That's very neat. But look now . . . if we lived in a state where virtue was profitable, common sense would make us good, and greed would make us saintly. And we'd live like animals or angels in the happy land that needs no heroes. But since in fact we see that avarice, anger, envy, pride, sloth, lust and stupidity commonly profit far beyond humility, chastity, fortitude, justice and thought, and have to choose, to be human at all . . . why then perhaps we must stand fast a little — even at the risk of being heroes.

MARGARET (*emotional*): But in reason! Haven't you done as much as God can reasonably want?

MORE: Well . . . finally . . . it isn't a matter of reason; finally it's a matter of love.

ALICE (*hostile*): You're content then, to be shut up here with mice and rats when you might be home with us!

MORE (*flinching*): Content? If they'd open a crack that wide (*between finger and thumb*) I'd be through it. (*To* MARGARET.) Well, has Eve run out of apples?

MARGARET: I've not yet told you what the house is like, without you.

MORE: Don't, Meg.

MARGARET: What we do in the evenings, now that you're not there.

MORE: Meg, have done!

MARGARET: We sit in the dark because we've no candles. And we've no talk because we're wondering what they're doing to you here.

MORE: The King's more merciful than you. He doesn't use the rack.

ROBERT BOLT

> The examiner will want to see that you have been able to analyse the relationships between More and his family, especially his daughter. What is the importance of the presents they bring, and how does their real motive for the visit contribute to the emotional and dramatic structure of the drama?
>
> More expresses important ideas in an almost Shakespearian fashion, i.e. with flourishes of rhetorical language, not intended to be realistic. Again, the examiner will look to see what you have made of these sections. There are important ideas about principle and morality in a world of injustice and insincerity.

ANSWER

Some of the emotional power of the passage comes about through the place where the conversation takes place. Sheer terror strikes us as a possible reaction to the way that Will Roper, on his way into the gaol, sees the rack, and we can also imagine the horror and dismal nature of More's solitary life when we learn about the dripping dampness of the cell, close to the river. These settings establish an emotional mood as well as the scene, one of misery and despair, although More is strong in the way that he shows himself not to be too bothered or downcast by the surroundings:

'Remarkably like any other place.'

Other emotions are brought out section by section through what the characters say to each other, and perhaps also through what lies beneath the surface of what they say.

Examiner's comment

It is helpful to comment on the setting whilst considering a work of drama. This has an effect on the themes and emotions. The candidate is talking about 'implication' when he mentions 'what lies beneath the surface', and although it would have been helpful if he had used the term, it is clearly recognised.

In the first place we see the delight that the prisoner feels at being able to see his family again:

More: (ecstatic, wraps her to him): 'Oh, good morning — Good morning.'

There is obviously great relief felt and a sense of emotional delight at More being reunited with his loved ones, although because Margaret is under oath to try and persuade him to swear to the Act of Succession, this spirit of open love and affection has to meet some difficulties as the scene continues. It is as if the rest of the scene involves the characters in trying to understand each others' positions and to learn all over again how to cope with a problem in the family. The emotions in the remainder of the extract are sometimes awkward, as if the characters do not understand each other.

Examiner's comment

Good general comment. Provided the essay continues to be well written, the examiner would now expect the candidate to move to more specific examples to show how this awkwardness in the emotions is established. In fact, with sound organisation, this candidate does this rather well, as you will see in the following paragraphs.

I think that when the family are handing him over the food and wine that they have brought, these are like emotional bribes, and there may be some hypocrisy in what they are doing. Rather than being straightforward, honest presents, they appear as some kind of hints of the world outside. This can be supported as a view when we see in the stage directions that his daughter, Margaret, cannot even look at him when she says:

'And, these other things . . .' (*She doesn't look at him.*)

Her embarrassment is caused by the fact that she knows that what she is doing is disloyal. She is under oath and the food and wine may be a way of trying to remind her father how much better life would be if he were prepared to sign away his principles and come back to them at home.

We then see an emotion of great disappointment, as Sir Thomas More feels so badly let down by what they are doing. The remainder of the passage is built around this emotion, when from this point on he has to try to convince them that what he is doing is right:

More: 'Is this why they let you come?'

Roper: 'Yes . . . Meg's under oath to persuade you.'

More (*coldly*): 'That was silly, Meg. How did you come to do that?'

This confrontation leads on to an understanding of the conflicting emotions felt by More and his family, which the dramatist goes on to explore in the remainder of the passage. The problem for the family is that they are suffering terribly without their husband and father, and however much he may feel that he is acting on an important principle, they are miserable at home. These emotions are brought out by Meg, who comes across as the more articulate of the two women, giving her father an idea of their suffering. She describes the way they spend their time, and this again is like moral blackmail. It is perhaps meant to contrast with his time in prison. Which is worse? The reader and audience are asked this question, although the answer has to be his life, because she is being so unfair on him:

'We sit in the dark because we've no candles. And we've no talk because we're wondering what they're doing to you here.'

In a climax of the emotions, More tells her off for such a method of persuading him, by saying:

'The King's more merciful than you. He doesn't use the rack.'

Overall, the writer establishes emotions which are not satisfactory between the family because of the difficulty of the situation they find themselves in. There are feelings of hostility and a kind of emotional bullying that is happening. In the end this is rather sad. Beneath all of this blackmail from his daughter, there may be a feeling which is part of the situation that this is a moment of great sadness for More, who is obviously going to stick to his principles, but is being put upon by the very people whom he ought to feel nearest to him, and from whom he should be able to seek support.

Examiner's comment

Excellent organisation has allowed for a clear analysis and summary of the emotions in the extract.

The second part of the question asks about ideas and themes. There are, as well as emotions, very strongly developed ideas about principles, use of language, and hope. Meg is trying to persuade More to 'swear to the Act of Succession'. The dramatist uses this attempt to persuade him, as a way to look at what is involved in swearing an oath, how we mean those words, and the truth and importance of them. More's view on the matter is quite simple:

'What is an oath then but words we say to God?'

Margaret feels that there is room for compromise on this principle. She takes the view that it is possible to say words, but hold a different, stronger view 'in your heart'. More uses a strong image to describe the way that people become compromised if they say what they do not mean. This is the image of the cupping of hands, and a person holding 'his own self in his own hands'. If you are without principle, you will let yourself drop through the hands, 'like water'.

The technique that the dramatist uses is to give these important words and ideas a great deal of prominence in the rhetorical speech of the main character. This is not very realistic, as we cannot easily imagine that a man facing his problems would be able to speak with such grace and ease, but he does so in the interests of making the ideas clear.

Examiner's comment

Good point about the way that the writer uses the form of the play in order to express major themes and ideas. The candidate is unable to state that this is part of the form of historical drama, but the important thing is that there is a recognition of how the form works.

The other main idea that comes across is the moral virtue of 'standing fast'. This does seem to be a main preoccupation of More as a character, and, again, it is strongly put over in a form of rhetoric which becomes convincing, like perhaps a political speech:

'But since in fact we see that avarice . . . and have to choose, to be human at all . . . why then perhaps we must stand fast a little — even at the risk of being heroes.'

It is important for More not just to refuse the oath, but also to make a stand for what is right and good, and therefore there are strong ideas and themes of moral goodness set against the evils of the world, in the passage.

There is also what looks like a religious idea emerging towards the end of the passage, when More states:

'Well . . . finally . . . it isn't a matter of reason; finally it's a matter of love.'

This could be that he is reasserting his love for the family, but, although the idea is not thoroughly dealt with, he is probably stating a love of God in these words.

As well as the ideas brought out above, of goodness and religion, there is one other important theme, which is the suffering. This is cleverly interwoven in a number of different ways in the text. First, there is the mention of the rack, which sets the scene for the kind of physical suffering that might happen to prisoners, but ironically here seems more to symbolise the emotional suffering that is going to happen to More in the scene. As the scene progresses, we see that More is not really suffering in prison at all. He is even quite content, perhaps because he feels he has right on his side. But the suffering at the hands of his family's emotional manipulation is acute, and so the reader is given a contrast between the physical suffering, and the mental, which is much worse for him, and against which he has to argue strongly. Add to that the suffering of loneliness for the family without their man, and we can soon see how successful the writer is at bringing this out as a theme.

My other feeling is that there is an underlying theme of imminent death, which could be termed 'hopelessness'. The presents come across to me as a final offering, and the whole conversation has the feel of being a last chance. More tries to put up a kind of false nature against this, as a way of remaining jocular even though he knows there is no hope.

Examiner's comment

This candidate is particularly well organised. He has moved through the passage sensibly, covering the emotions, ideas and themes in some detail. He has also been prepared to offer suggestions that can only be hinted from the extract, without fuller knowledge of the play. Throughout, he has been interpretive and analytical, which has led to a close understanding of themes and ideas.

5 Exam practice

This unit presents you with a number of tasks which you are invited to use for practice. The first tasks are deliberately chosen from actual and specimen papers which have been produced by the different Examination Boards. The later tasks have been compiled using a variety of stimuli with a similar style of questioning. Each example is accompanied by an examiner's tip which will give you some insight into the way in which the task might be approached. You might choose to plan an answer before reading the tip.

Before attempting any of the questions, you should consider the following criteria, which have been taken from the mark scheme of one Examining Board.

'Throughout the mark range we should look to reward evidence of:

- careful analysis of content and expression;
- independent opinion and evaluation, when this is supported by evidence from the text;
- awareness, where appropriate, of audience and purpose;
- awareness of context, including period conditions, characteristics, style and vocabulary;
- awareness of the characteristics and exigencies of genre and form;
- sensitivity to the use of language: vocabulary, tone, nuance, implication, ambiguity;
- knowledgeable use (as opposed to mere display) of critical terms;
- clarity, precision and felicity of expression.'

This list is worth keeping in mind at all times and is applicable to all Examining Boards.

TASK 1

The following extract comes from the novel *Wide Sargasso Sea*, (1966) in which Jean Rhys imagines the early history of the girl who was to become Mr Rochester's mad wife in Charlotte Brontë's *Jane Eyre*. The passage centres on a conversation that takes place soon after their marriage when they are staying on her family estate in the Windward Islands. The novel is set in the 1830s. The narrator at this point is Rochester.

What is the author concerned to do in this passage and what means does she employ to do it?

EXTRACT

Wide Sargasso Sea

The long veranda was furnished with canvas chairs, two hammocks, and a wooden table on which stood a tripod telescope. Amélie brought out candles with glass shades but the night swallowed up the feeble light. There was a very strong scent of flowers — the flowers by the river that open at night she told me — and the noise, subdued in the inner room, was deafening. 'Cric-cracs,' she explained, 'they make a sound like their name, and crickets and frogs.'

I leaned on the railing and saw hundreds of fireflies — 'Ah yes, fireflies in Jamaica, here they call a firefly La belle.'

A large moth, so large that I thought it was a bird, blundered into one of the candles, put it out and fell to the floor. 'He's a big fellow,' I said.

'Is it badly burned?'

'More stunned than hurt.'

I took the beautiful creature up in my handkerchief and put it on the railing. For a moment it was still and by the dim candlelight I could see the soft brilliant colours, the intricate pattern on the wings. I shook the handkerchief gently and it flew away.

'I hope that gay gentleman will be safe,' I said.

'He will come back if we don't put the candles out. It's light enough by the stars.'

Indeed the starlight was so bright that shadows of the veranda posts and the trees outside lay on the floor.

'Now come for a walk,' she said, 'and I will tell you a story.'

We walked along the veranda to the steps which led to the lawn.

'We used to come here to get away from the hot weather in June, July and August. I came three times with my Aunt Cora who is ill. That was after . . .'. She stopped and put her hand up to her head.

'If this is a sad story, don't tell it to me tonight.'

'It is not sad,' she said. 'Only some things happen and are there for always even though you forget why or when. It was in that little bedroom.'

I looked where she was pointing but could only see the outline of a narrow bed and one or two chairs.

'This night I can remember it was very hot. The window was shut but I asked Christophine to open it because the breeze comes from the hills at night. The land breeze. Not from the sea. It was so hot that my night chemise was sticking to me but I went to sleep all the same. And then suddenly I was awake. I saw two enormous rats, as big as cats, on the sill staring at me.'

'I'm not astonished that you were frightened.'

'But I was not frightened. That was the strange thing. I stared at them and they did not move. I could see myself in the looking-glass the other side of the room, in my white chemise with a frill round the neck, staring at those rats and the rats quite still, staring at me.'

'Well, what happened?'

'I turned over, pulled up the sheet, and went to sleep instantly.'

'And that is the story?'

'No, I woke up again suddenly like the first time and the rats were not there but I felt very frightened. I got out of bed quickly and ran on to the veranda. I lay down in this hammock. This one.' She pointed to a flat hammock, a rope at each of the four corners.

'There was a full moon that night — and I watched it for a long time. There were no clouds chasing it, so it seemed to be standing still and it shone on me. Next morning Christophine was angry. She said it was very bad to sleep in the moonlight when the moon is full.'

'And did you tell her about the rats?'

'No, I never told anyone till now. But I have never forgotten them.'

I wanted to say something reassuring but the scent of the river flowers was overpoweringly strong. I felt giddy.

'Do you think that too,' she said, 'that I have slept too long in the moonlight?'

Her mouth was set in a fixed smile but her eyes were so withdrawn and lonely that I put my arms around her, rocked her like a child and sang to her. An old song I thought I had forgotten:

'Hail to the queen of the silent night,
Shine bright, shine bright Robin as you die.'

She listened, then sang with me:

'Shine bright, shine bright Robin as you die.'

There was no one in the house and only two candles in the room which had been so brilliantly lit. Her room was dim, with a shaded candle by the bed and another on the dressing-table. There was a bottle of wine on the round table. It was very late when I poured out two glasses and told her to drink to our happiness, to our love and the day without end which would be tomorrow. I was young then. A short youth mine was.

JEAN RHYS

Oxford

TASK 2

Write a careful critical appraisal of the following poem, *Ritornello*, by Charles Tomlinson (b. 1927), showing what the poet is saying and the connection between that and how he chooses to say it.

In your answer you may find it useful to comment on the impact of the verse form, the choice and ordering of words, and the sounds and rhythms.

POEM

Ritornello

Wrong has a twisty look like wrung misprinted
Consider! and you con the stars for meaning
Sublime comes climbing from beneath the threshold
Experience? you win it out of peril
The pirate's cognate. Where did the words arise?
Human they sublimed out of the humus.
Surprised by stars into consideration
You are wrung right and put into the peril
Of feelings not yet charted lost for words
Abstraction means something pulled away from
Humus means earth place purchase and return.

CHARLES TOMLINSON

Oxford

TASK 3

Compare and contrast the following poems: *Since There's no Help* by Michael Drayton (1561–1631) and *Out of Danger* by James Fenton (b. 1949). Among other points, you should consider the way each poet uses his chosen form to control the tone of his poem.

POEM *(a)*

Since There's no Help

Since there's no help, come let us kiss and part:
Nay, I have done; you get no more of me;
And I am glad, yea, glad with all my heart
That thus so cleanly I myself can free.
Shake hands forever; cancel all our vows;
And when we meet at any time again,
Be it not seen in either of our brows
That we one jot of former love retain.
Now at the last gasp of Love's latest breath
When, his pulse failing, Passion speechless lies,
When Faith is kneeling by his bed of death
And Innocence is closing up his eyes;
Now, if thou would'st, when all have given him over,
From Death to Life thou might'st him yet recover.

MICHAEL DRAYTON

POEM *(b)*

Out of Danger

Heart be kind and sign the release
As the trees their loss approve.
Learn as leaves must learn to fall
Out of danger, out of love.

What belongs to frost and thaw
Sullen winter will not harm.
What belongs to wind and rain
Is out of danger from the storm.

Jealous passion, cruel need
Betray the heart they feed upon
But what belongs to earth and death
Is out of danger from the sun.

I was cruel, I was wrong —
Hard to say and hard to know.
You do not belong to me.
You are out of danger now.

Out of danger from the wind,
Out of danger from the wave,
Out of danger from the heart
Falling, falling out of love.

JAMES FENTON

UCLES

John Mortimer's play *A Voyage Round my Father* was first performed in 1970. Explore the dramatic presentation and effect of this passage from the play, commenting on any technical features (stage directions, for example) that seem to you significant.

TASK 4

A Voyage Round my Father

EXTRACT

The Father enters in his garden hat, his hand on the Mother's arm.

FATHER: Rhododendrons out?

MOTHER: Yes, dear.

FATHER: A fine show of rhododendrons . . . and the little syringa?

MOTHER: Just out.

FATHER: Just out. And smelling sweetly. Azaleas doing well?

MOTHER: You can see they're a little brown, round the edges.

FATHER: Azaleas doing moderately well . . . Our visitor here?

MOTHER: Yes, dear. Elizabeth's here.

FATHER: Is that you?

SON: We're both here.

FATHER: Is your visitor enjoying the garden?

ELIZABETH: Quite well. Thank you.

FATHER: I've often wondered about my son. Does he treat girls well . . . ?

SON: Why've you wondered that?

FATHER: I once knew a man named Arthur Pennycuick. Like you in some ways. He didn't treat girls well . . .

MOTHER: Please, dear . . . Arthur Pennycuick's not suitable.

ELIZABETH: Tell us. What did he do to girls?

FATHER: When I was a young man, I was out with this Pennycuick. And he picked up a girl. In the promenade of the old Empire Music Hall. And before he went off with her, he took off his cufflinks and gave them to me for safekeeping. In her *presence*! I felt so sick and angry, seeing him take out his old gold cufflinks. I never spoke to him again. Disgusting!

ELIZABETH: *You* think if you sleep with someone — you should trust them with your cufflinks?

FATHER: At least not take them out — *in front of the girl*! Well, we can see a fine show of rhododendrons.

MOTHER: Yes, and I must show you the polyanthas.

FATHER: A reward at last, for a good deal of tedious potting up.

ELIZABETH [*impatient, as letting out something she's kept bottled up for a long time*]: Why do you bother?

FATHER: What?

ELIZABETH: I said why do you bother to do all this gardening? I mean when you can't see it?

Both the Mother and the Son try to interrupt her, protectively.

MOTHER: My dear . . .

SON: Elizabeth . . .

ELIZABETH: Well he can't see it, can he? Why do you walk about — pretending he's not blind?

The Father shakes off the Mother's arm and moves, his hand out in front of him, towards Elizabeth. He gets to her: touches her arm, feels down her arm, and puts his in it.

FATHER: Is that you?

ELIZABETH: Yes . . .

FATHER: Would you take me to West Copse? I'd like . . . a report on the magnolia. Would you do that? [*Pause.*] Be my eyes.

Elizabeth looks up at him, suspicious, not quite understanding what he's up to. Then she says, almost brutally:

ELIZABETH: Come on then . . .

She moves away, with the Father on her arm.

JOHN MORTIMER
UCLES

TASK 5

Write a critical appreciation of the following work by Isaac Rosenberg, a poet-soldier in the trenches during World War One (1914–1918). He mentions two experiences, picking a poppy and seeing a rat, which lead him to reflect upon his situation. You should comment on such matters as theme, imagery, development of ideas, tone and use of language.

POEM

Break of Day in the Trenches

The darkness crumbles away.
It is the same old Druid Time as ever,
Only a live thing leaps my hand,
A queer sardonic rat —
As I pull the parapet's poppy
To stick behind my ear.
Droll rat, they would shoot you if they knew
Your cosmopolitan sympathies.
Now you have touched this English hand
You will do the same to a German,
Soon, no doubt, if it be your pleasure
To cross the sleeping green between.
It seems you inwardly grin as you pass
Strong eyes, fine limbs, haughty athletes
Less chanced than you for life,
Bonds to the whims of murder,

Sprawled in the bowels of the earth,
The torn fields of France.
What do you see in our eyes
At the shrieking iron and flame
Hurled still through heavens?
What quaver — what heart aghast?
Poppies whose roots are in man's veins
Drop, and are ever dropping:
But mine in my ear is safe —
Just a little white with dust.

ISAAC ROSENBERG

NEAB

This piece is the beginning of Anita Brookner's *Hotel du Lac* (1984), set in a lakeside hotel in Switzerland. You may write about it in whatever way you wish, yet you may want to consider the following:

 TASK 6

- the personality of the Edith Hope character;
- the mood and atmosphere, particularly in the first and third paragraphs;
- the impact of the passage as an opening to a novel.

Hotel du Lac

EXTRACT

From the window all that could be seen was a receding area of grey. It was to be supposed that beyond the grey garden, which seemed to sprout nothing but the stiffish leaves of some unfamiliar plant, lay the vast grey lake, spreading like an anaesthetic towards the invisible further shore, and beyond that, in imagination only, yet verified by the brochure, the peak of Dent d'Oche, on which snow might already be slightly and silently falling. For it was late September, out of season; the tourists had gone, the rates were reduced, and there were few inducements for visitors in this small town at the water's edge, whose inhabitants, uncommunicative to begin with, were frequently rendered taciturn by the dense cloud that descended for days at a time and then vanished without warning to reveal a new landscape, full of colour and incident: boats skimming on the lake, passengers at the landing stage, an open air market, the outline of the gaunt remains of a thirteenth-century castle, seams of white on the far mountains, and on the cheerful uplands to the south a rising backdrop of apple trees, the fruit sparkling with emblematic significance. For this was a land of prudently harvested plenty, a land which had conquered human accidents, leaving only the weather distressingly beyond control.

Edith Hope, a writer of romantic fiction under a more thrusting name, remained standing at the window, as if an access of goodwill could pierce the mysterious opacity with which she had been presented, although she had been promised a tonic cheerfulness, a climate devoid of illusions, an utterly commonsensical set of circumstances — quiet hotel, excellent cuisine, long walks, lack of excitement, early nights — in which she could be counted upon to retrieve her serious and hard-working personality and to forget the unfortunate lapse which had led to this brief exile, in this apparently unpopulated place, at this slowly darkening time of the year, when she should have been at home . . . . But it was home, or, rather, 'home', which had become inimical all at once, so that she had acquiesced, rather frightened at what was happening to her, when her friends had suggested a short break, and had allowed herself to be driven to the airport by her friend and neighbour, Penelope Milne, who, tight-lipped, was prepared to forgive her only on condition that she disappeared for a decent length of time and came back older, wiser, and properly apologetic. For I am not

 Letts **Q&A**

to be allowed my lapse, as if I were an artless girl, she thought: and why should I be? I am a serious woman who should know better and am judged by my friends to be past the age of indiscretion. I am a householder, a ratepayer, a good plain cook, and a deliverer of typescripts well before the deadline: I sign anything that is put in front of me; I never telephone my publisher: and I make no claims for my particular sort of writing, although I understand that it is doing quite well. I have held this rather dim and trusting personality together for a considerable length of time, and although I have certainly bored others I was not to be allowed to bore myself. My profile was deemed to be low and it was agreed by those who thought they knew me that it should stay that way. And no doubt after a curative stay in this grey solitude (and I notice that the leaves of that plant are quite immobile) I shall be allowed back, to resume my peaceable existence, and to revert to what I was before I did that apparently dreadful thing, although, frankly, once I had done it I didn't give it another thought. But I do now. Yes.

Turning her back on the toneless expanse beyond the window, she contemplated the room, which was the colour of over-cooked veal: veal-coloured carpet and curtains, high, narrow bed with veal-coloured counterpane, small austere table with a correct chair placed tightly underneath it, a narrow wardrobe, and at a very great height above her head, a tiny brass chandelier, which, she knew, would eventually twinkle drearily with eight weak bulbs. Stiff white lace curtains, providing even more protection against the sparse daylight, could be parted to allow access, through long windows, to a narrow strip of balcony on which were placed a green metal table and chair. I shall be able to write there when the weather is fine, she thought . . . .

ANITA BROOKNER

NEAB

TASK 7 The following two poems are both by Edward Thomas (1878–1917). Compare and contrast the poems, considering in particular the diction, movement and emotional impact of each one.

POEM (a)   *It Rains*

> It rains, and nothing stirs within the fence
> Anywhere through the orchard's untrodden, dense
> Forest of parsley. The great diamonds
> Of rain on the grassblades there is none to break
> Or the fallen petals further down to shake.
>
> And I am nearly as happy as possible
> To search the wilderness in vain though well,
> To think of two walking, kissing there,
> Drenched, yet forgetting the kisses of the rain:
> Sad, too, to think that never, never again,
>
> Unless alone, so happy shall I walk
> In the rain. When I turned away, on its fine stalk
> Twilight has fined to naught, the parsley flower
> Figures, suspended still and ghostly white,
> The past hovering as it revisits the light.

EDWARD THOMAS

(b) *After Rain*

The rain of a night and a day and a night
Stops at the light
Of this pale choked day. The peering sun
Sees what has been done.
The road under the trees has a border new
Of purple hue
Inside the border of bright thin grass:
For all that has
Been left by November of leaves is torn
From hazel and thorn
And the greater trees. Throughout the copse
No dead leaf drops
On grey grass, green moss, burnt-orange fern,
At the wind's return:
The leaflets out of the ash-tree shed
Are thinly spread
In the road, like little black fish, inlaid,
As if they played.
What hangs from the myriad branches down there
So hard and bare
Is twelve yellow apples lovely to see
On one crab-tree.
And on each twig of every tree in the dell
Uncountable
Crystals both dark and bright of the rain
That begins again.

EDWARD THOMAS

NEAB

Explore the similarities and the differences in the ways Thomas Hardy and Carol Ann Duffy present the breakdown of a relationship in the two poems which follow.

You will need to spend a substantial proportion of your time reading the material and preparing and planning your answers.

(a) *Neutral Tones*

We stood by a pond that winter day,
And the sun was white, as though chidden of God,
And a few leaves lay on the starving sod;
— They had fallen from an ash, and were grey.

Your eyes on me were as eyes that rove
Over tedious riddles of years ago;
And words played between us to and fro —
On which lost the more by our love.

The smile on your mouth was the deadest thing
Alive enough to have strength to die;
And a grin of bitterness swept thereby
Like an ominous bird a-wing . . .

Since then, keen lessons that love deceives,
And wrings with wrong, have shaped to me
Your face, and the God-curst sun, and a tree,
And a pond edged with grayish leaves.

THOMAS HARDY

POEM *(b)* *Disgrace*

But one day we woke to disgrace; our house
a coldness of rooms, each nursing
a thickening cyst of dust and gloom.
We had not been home in our hearts for months.

And how our words changed. Dead flies in a web.
How they stiffened and blackened. Cherished italics
suddenly sour on our tongues, obscenities
spraying themselves on the wall in my head.

Woke to your clothes like a corpse on the floor,
the small deaths of lightbulbs pining all day
in my ears, their echoes audible tears;
nothing we would not do to make it worse

and worse. Into the night with the wrong language,
waving and pointing, the shadows of hands
huge in the bedroom. Dreamed of a naked crawl
from a dead place over the other; both of us. Woke.

Woke to the absence of grace; the still-life
of a meal, untouched, wine-bottle, empty, ashtray,
full. In our sullen kitchen, the fridge
hardened its cold heart, selfish as art, hummed.

To a bowl of apples rotten to the core. Lame shoes
empty in the hall where our voices asked
for a message after the tone, the telephone
pressing its ear to the distant, invisible lips.

And our garden bowing its head, vulnerable flowers
unseen in the dusk as we shouted in silhouette.
Woke to the screaming alarm, the banging door,
the house-plants trembling in their brittle soil. Total

disgrace. Up in the dark to stand at the window,
counting the years to arrive there, faithless,
unpenitent. Woke to the meaningless stars, you
and me both, lost. Inconsolable vowels from the next room.

CAROL ANN DUFFY

AEB

TASK 9

The following two extracts are from *City of the Mind* by Penelope Lively and *Hawksmoor* by Peter Ackroyd, both written this century. Read both extracts carefully several times, and then write about the ways that the writers present:

(a) the nature of the city;

(b) the relationship of the man with the city.

(a)

City of the Mind

And thus, driving through the city, he is both here and now, there and then. He carries yesterday with him, but pushes forward into today, and tomorrow, skipping as he will from one to the other. He is in London, on a May morning of the late twentieth century, but he is also in many other places, and at other times. He twitches the knob of his radio: New York speaks to him, five hours ago, is superseded by Australia tomorrow and presently by India this evening. He learns of events that have not yet taken place, of deaths that have not yet occurred. He is Matthew Halland, an English architect stuck in a traffic jam, a person of no great significance, and yet omniscient. For him, the world no longer turns; there is no day or night, everything and everywhere are instantaneous. He forges his way along Euston Road, in fits and starts, speeding up, then clogged again between panting taxis and a lorry with a churning wasp-striped cement mixer. He is both trapped, and ranging free. He fiddles again with the radio, runs through a lexicon of French song, Arab exhortation, invective in some language he cannot identify. Halted once more, he looks sideways and meets the thoughtful gaze of Jane Austen (1785–1817), ten feet high on a poster, improbably teamed with Isambard Kingdom Brunel and George Frederick Handel, all of them dead, gone, but doing well — live and kicking in his head and up there guarding the building site that will become the British Library. And then another car cuts ahead of his, he hoots, accelerates, is channelled on in another licensed burst of speed. Jane Austen is replaced by St Pancras.

Thus he coasts through the city, his body in one world and his head in many. He is told so much, and from so many sources, that he has learned to disregard, to let information filter through the mind and vanish, leaving impressions — a phrase, a fact, an image. He knows much, and very little. He knows more than he can confront; his wisdoms have blunted his sensibility. He is an intelligent man, and a man of compassion, but he can hear of a massacre on the other side of the globe and wonder as he listens if he remembered to switch on his answering machine. He is aware of this, and is disturbed.

The city, too, bombards him. He sees decades and centuries, poverty and wealth, grace and vulgarity. He sees a kaleidoscope of time and mood: buildings that ape Gothic cathedrals, that remember Greek temples, that parade symbols and images. He sees columns, pediments and porticos. He sees Victorian stucco, twentieth-century concrete, a snatch of Georgian brick. He notes the resilience and tenacity of the city, and its indifference.

PENELOPE LIVELY

(b)

Hawksmoor

Hawksmoor could have produced a survey of the area between the two churches of Wapping and Limehouse, and given at the same time a precise account of the crimes which each quarter harboured. This had been the district of the CID to which he had been attached for some years, before he was assigned to the Murder Squad, and he had come to know it well: he knew where the thieves lived, where the prostitutes gathered, and where the vagrants came. He grew to understand that most criminals tend to remain in the same districts, continuing with their activities until they were arrested, and he sometimes speculated that these same areas had been used with similar intent for centuries past: even murderers, who rapidly became Hawksmoor's speciality, rarely moved from the same spot but killed again and again until they were discovered. And sometimes he speculated, also, that they were drawn to those places where murders had occurred before. In his own time in this district, there had been a house in Red Maiden Lane in which three separate murders had been perpetrated over a period of eight years, and the building itself gave such an impression to those who entered it that it had stayed unoccupied since the last killing. In Swedenborg Gardens Robert Haynes had murdered his wife and child, and it was Hawksmoor who was called when the remains were found beneath the floorboards; in Commercial Road there had been the ritual slaying of one Catherine Hayes, and then only last year a certain Thomas Berry had been stabbed and then mutilated in the alley beside St George's-in-the-East. It had been in this district, as Hawksmoor knew, that the Marr murders of 1812 had occurred — the perpetrator being a certain John Williams, who, according to De Quincey whose account Hawksmoor avidly read, 'asserted his own supremacy above all the children of Cain.' He killed four in a house by Ratcliffe Highway — a man, wife, servant and child — by shattering their skulls with a mallet and then gratuitously cutting their throats as they lay dying. Then, twelve days later and in the same quarter, he repeated his acts upon another family. He was transformed, again according to De Quincey, into a 'mighty murderer' and until his execution he remained an object of awe and mystery to those who lived in the shadow of the Wapping church. The mob tried to dismember his body when eventually it was brought in a cart to the place of burial — at the conflux of four roads in front of the church, where he was interred and a stake driven through his heart. And, as far as Hawksmoor knew, he lay there still: it was the spot where he had this morning seen the crowd pressing against the cordon set up by the police.

PETER ACKROYD

AEB

TASK 10

Write a critical appreciation of the following poem, *Carousel*, by the West Indian poet Lucinda Roy. How effectively and by what means does she express feelings of loss and affection through her writing?

POEM

Carousel
(For Namba Roy, 1910–1961)

I often spin around with you and hear
the fragile music of a carousel;
I feel your black arms round me in a heavy sweep
of closeness, taking me up on notes which fall
like eggs through water.

       I am older now
and you have fallen from the garish horse
a long time since, and I am holding on
with thin brown fingers. Do you know
it's been a quarter of a century since you
(with your voice like the man who plays God in the movies)
kissed me? I don't remember your kisses.
I remember you wearing striped pyjamas
and waving to me from the ward — your great hand
scooping a half-circle out of nothing;
how my brother almost choked on a *Lifesaver*
until a male nurse turned him upside down
and out came the white mint with the hole
that saved him.

       I dreamed you died, and when I woke
my mother was by the bed. 'How will I light
the fire?' she said. I didn't know.
It was cold in our house; our breath came out
round as balloons and dissolved till we breathed
again. We learned to accommodate spaces

as you must have learned to accommodate . . .
but no. Where there is no place to put things,
no place for your bones or your slippers or my words
there cannot be a place for spaces.
It must be fine to know only lack of substance —
the round emptiness in an angel's trumpet —
and still hear music.

I have the things you made
and she has made us see you in them.
I have the ivory statues and the pictures
telling stories of African ancestors,
a birth, flights into Egypt. In your work
I find the stillness of your eyes and mouth,
the stillness which is always at the centre
of the spinning ball we hurl high and long.
I often spin around with you and hear
the fragile music of a carousel.
My horse would gallop forward if I let him
but I prefer the swinging back to where
we were, slow undulations round and back
to identical place. I prefer to see
your black hands with mine on a crimson mane
which will never be swept back by the wind.

LUCINDA ROY

UCLES

In the following extract from Shakespeare's play *Pericles* (c.1609) Pericles, Prince of Tyre, is at sea during a violent storm. Lychorida, a nurse, enters with his new-born child. Write a commentary on the passage, discussing in particular the way Shakespeare handles the dramatic presentation of character and incident.

TASK 11

Pericles

EXTRACT

Enter PERICLES, *on shipboard.*

PERICLES: Thou god of this great vast, rebuke these surges,
Which wash both heaven and hell; and thou that hast
Upon the winds command, bind them in brass,
Having call'd them from the deep! O, still
Thy deaf'ning, dreadful thunders; gently quench
Thy nimble sulphurous flashes! O, how, Lychorida,
How does my queen? Thou stormest venomously;
Wilt thou spit all thyself? The seaman's whistle
Is as a whisper in the ears of death,
Unheard. Lychorida! — Lucina, O
Divinest patroness, and midwife gentle
To those that cry by night, convey thy deity
Aboard our dancing boat; make swift the pangs
Of my queen's travails! Now, Lychorida!

Enter LYCHORIDA, *[with an infant].*

LYCHORIDA: Here is a thing too young for such a place,
Who, if it had conceit, would die, as I

85

PERICLES: Am like to do. Take in your arms this piece
Of your dead queen.

PERICLES: How? How, Lychorida?

LYCHORIDA: Patience, good sir; do not assist the storm.
Here's all that is left living of your queen,
A little daughter: for the sake of it,
Be manly, and take comfort.

PERICLES: O you gods!
Why do you make us love your goodly gifts,
And snatch them straight away? We here below
Recall not what we give, and therein may
Vie in honour with you.

LYCHORIDA: Patience, good sir,
Even for this charge.

PERICLES: Now, mild may be thy life!
For a more blusterous birth had never babe;
Quiet and gentle thy conditions! for
Thou are the rudeliest welcome to this world
That e'er was prince's child. Happy what follows!
Thou hast as chiding a nativity
As fire, air, water, earth, and heaven can make,
To herald thee from the womb. (Poor inch of nature!)
Even at the first thy loss is more than can
Thy portage quit, with all thou canst find here.
Now the good gods throw their best eyes upon't!

WILLLIAM SHAKESPEARE

UCLES

TASK 12

The book from which this extract is taken is very largely about literary criticism and you are invited in it to consider techniques which you need to employ in your own work.

This passage by T S Eliot is from an essay on criticism which he wrote in 1933. Carefully analyse what he is saying about literary criticism and continue with an expression of your personal view on what he says.

EXTRACT

The Function of Criticism

From time to time, every hundred years or so, it is desirable that some critic shall appear to review the past of our literature, and set the poets and the poems in a new order. This task is not one of revolution but of readjustment. What we observe is partly the same scene, but in a different and more distant perspective; there are new and strange objects in the foreground, to be drawn accurately in proportion to the more familiar ones which now approach the horizon, where all but the most eminent become invisible to the naked eye. The exhaustive critic, armed with a powerful glass, will be able to sweep the distance and gain an acquaintance with minute objects in the landscape with which to compare minute objects close at hand; he will be able to gauge nicely the position and proportion of the objects surrounding us, in the whole of the vast panorama. This metaphorical fancy only represents the ideal; but Dryden, Johnson, and Arnold have each performed the task as well as human frailty will allow. The majority of critics can be expected only to parrot the opinions of the last master of criticism; among more independent minds a period of destruction, of preposterous over-examination, and of successive fashions takes place. until a new authority comes to introduce some order. And it is not merely the passage of time and accumulation of new artistic experience, nor the ineradicable tendency of the great majority of men to repeat the opinions of those few who have taken the trouble to think, nor the tendency of a nimble but myopic minority to progenerate heterodoxies, that makes new assessments necessary. It is that no generation is interested in Art in quite the same way as any other; each generation, like each individual, brings to the contemplation of art its own categories of appreciation, makes its own demands upon art, and has its own uses for art. Pure artistic appreciation is to my thinking only an ideal, when not merely a figment, and must be, so long as the appreciation of art is an affair of limited and transient human beings existing in space and time. Both artist and audience are limited. There is for each time, for each artist, a kind of alloy required to make the metal workable into art; and each generation prefers its own alloy to any other. Hence each new master of criticism performs a useful service merely by the fact that his errors are of a different kind from the last; and the longer the sequence of critics we have, the greater amount of correction is possible.

T S ELIOT

Write a commentary on the following passage from *Samson Agonistes* by John Milton (1671). Does Milton achieve a genuinely dramatic atmosphere?

TASK 13

EXTRACT

Samson Agonistes

SAMSON: My wife, my traitress, let her come not near me.

CHORUS: Yet on she moves, now stands and eyes thee fixed,
About t' have spoke; but now, with head declined
Like a fair flower surcharged with dew, she weeps,
And words addressed seem into tears dissolved,
Wetting the borders of her silken veil;
But now again she makes address to speak.

DELILA: With doubtful feet and wavering resolution
I came, still dreading thy displeasure, Samson,
Which to have merited, without excuse,
I cannot but acknowledge; yet if tears
May expiate (though the fact more evil drew
In the perverse event than I foresaw),
My penance hath not slackened, though my pardon
No way assured. But conjugal affection,
Prevailing over fear and timorous doubt,
Hath led me on, desirous to behold
Once more thy face, and know of thy estate;
If aught in my ability may serve
To lighten what thou suffer'st, and appease
Thy mind with what amends is in my power,
Though late, yet in some part to recompense
My rash but more unfortunate misdeed.

SAMSON: Out, out, hyena! These are thy wonted arts,
And arts of every woman false like thee,
To break all faith, all vows, deceive, betray;
Then as repentant to submit, beseech,
And reconcilement move with feigned remorse,
Confess, and promise wonders in her change,
Not truly penitent, but chief to try

Her husband, how far urged his patience bears,
His virtue or weakness which way to assail;
Then with more cautious and instructed skill
Again transgresses, and again submits;
That wisest and best men, full oft beguiled,
With goodness principled not to reject
The penitent, but ever to forgive,
Are drawn to wear out miserable days,
Entangled with a poisonous bosom snake,
If not by quick destruction soon cut off,
As I by thee, to ages an example.

JOHN MILTON
UCLES

TASK 14

Write a commentary on this passage (1966), examining in particular the author's handling of character and situation.

EXTRACT

The Jewel in the Crown

Kumar moved away from the unattended counter and took up a position from which he judged he would be able to catch the assistant's eye. He was right. He did. But the assistant's expression was that of someone who did not remember ever having been spoken to about Pears' soap. Kumar wished that the assistant's new customers had been men. He could have interrupted their conversation, then, without putting himself in the wrong. Instead, he found himself in the ignominious role of watcher on the sidelines, in a situation another man was taking advantage of: hiding, as Kumar put it to himself, behind the skirts of a group of women. He looked around and saw the man who had come from the dispensary going back there. He said to him, 'I asked someone if you had any Pears' soap.'

The man stopped: perhaps because Kumar's voice automatically arrested him with its sahib-inflexions. Momentarily he seemed to be at a loss, assessing the evidence of his eyes and the evidence of his ears. 'Pears'?' he said at last. 'Oh yes, we have Pears'. Who is it for?'

It was a question Kumar had not expected, and one he did not immediately understand. But then did. Who did this fellow think he was? Some babu shopping for his master?

'Well, it's for me, naturally,' he said.

'One dozen or two dozen?'

Kumar's mouth was dry.

'One bar,' he said, trying to be dignified about it.

'We only sell it by the dozen,' the man explained, 'but you could get it in the bazaar, I expect,' and then added something in Hindi, which Kumar did not understand.

He said, 'I'm sorry. I don't speak Hindi. What are you trying to say?'

And was conscious, now, that because he was annoyed he had raised his voice, and other people in the shop were watching and listening. He caught the eye of one of the Englishwomen. Slowly she turned away with a smile he could only attach two words to: bitter, contemptuous.

'I was saying,' the man replied, 'that if you are only wanting one bar of Pears' soap you will find it cheaper in the Chillianwallah Bazaar because there they are taking no notice of regulated retail prices.'

'Thank you,' Kumar said, 'you have been most helpful,' and walked out.

PAUL SCOTT
UCLES

Write a critical appreciation of **one** of the following passages, *Song: Squats on a Toad-stool* by Thomas Beddoes (1803–49) and *That in Aleppo Once* by Vladimir Nabokov (1899–1977).

(a)   *Song: Squats on a Toad-stool*

Squats on a toad-stool under a tree
A bodiless childfull of life in the gloom,
Crying with frog voice, 'What shall I be?
Poor unborn ghost, for my mother killed me
Scarcely alive in her wicked womb.
What shall I be? shall I creep to the egg
That's cracking asunder yonder by Nile,
And with eighteen toes,
And a snuff-taking nose,
Make an Egyptian crocodile?
Sing, 'Catch a mummy by the leg
And crunch him with an upper jaw,
Wagging tail and clenching claw;
Take a bill-full from my craw,
Neighbour raven, caw, O caw,
grunt, my crocky, pretty maw!'

'Swine, shall I be one? 'Tis a dear dog;
But for a smile, and kiss, and pout,
I much prefer your black-lipped snout,
Little, gruntless, fairy hog,
Godson of the hawthorn hedge.
For, when Ringwood snuffs me out,
And 'gins my tender paunch to grapple,
Sing, ' 'Twixt your ancles visage wedge,
And roll up like an apple.'

'Serpent Lucifer, how do you do?
Of your worms and your snakes I'd be one or two
For in this dear planet of wool and leather
'Tis pleasant to need no shirt, breeches or shoe,
And have arm, leg, and belly together.
Then aches round your head, or are you lazy?
Sing, 'Round your neck your belly wrap,
Tail-a-top, and make your cap
Any bee and daisy.'

'I'll not be a fool, like a nightingale
Who sits up all midnight without any ale.
Making a noise with his nose;
Nor a camel, although 'tis a beautiful back;
nor a duck, notwithstanding the music of quack
And the webby, mud-patting toes.
I'll be a new bird with the head of an ass,
Two pigs' feet, two men's feet, and two of a hen;
Devil-winged; dragon-bellied; grave-jawed, because grass
Is a beard that's soon shaved, and grows seldom again
Before it is summer; so cow all the rest;
The new Dodo is finished. O! come to my nest.'

                                    THOMAS BEDDOES

EXTRACT *(b)*

That in Aleppo Once

I married, let me see, about a month after you left France and a few weeks before the gentle Germans roared into Paris. Although I can produce documentary proofs of matrimony, I am positive now that my wife never existed. You may know her name from some other source, but that does not matter: it is the name of an illusion. Therefore, I am able to speak of her with as much detachment as I would of a character in a story (one of your stories, to be precise).

It was love at first touch rather than at first sight, for I had met her several times before without experiencing any special emotions; but one night, as I was seeing her home, something quaint she had said made me stoop with a laugh and lightly kiss her on the hair — and of course we all know of that blinding blast which is caused by merely picking up a small doll from the floor of a carefully abandoned house: the soldier involved hears nothing; for him it is but an ecstatic soundless and boundless expansion of what had been during his life a pin-point of light in the dark centre of his being. And really, the reason we think of death in celestial terms is that the visible firmament, especially at night (above our blacked-out Paris with the gaunt arches of its Boulevard Exelmans and the ceaseless Alpine gargle of desolate latrines), is the most adequate and ever-present symbol of that vast silent explosion.

But I cannot discern her. She remains as nebulous as my best poem — the one you made such gruesome fun of in the Literaturnie Zapiski. When I want to imagine her, I have to cling mentally to a tiny brown birthmark on her downy forearm, as one concentrates upon a punctuation mark in an illegible sentence. Perhaps, had she used a great amount of make-up or used it more constantly, I might have visualised her face today, or at least the delicate transverse furrows of dry, hot rouged lips; but I fail, I fail — although I still feel their elusive touch now and then in the blindman's buff of my senses, in that sobbing sort of dream when she and I clumsily catch at each other through a heart-breaking mist and I cannot see the colour of her eyes for the blank lustre of brimming tears drowning their irises.

She was much younger than I — not as much younger as was Natalie of the lovely bare shoulders and long ear-rings in relation to swarthy Pushkin; but still there was a sufficient margin for that kind of retrospective romanticism which finds pleasure in imitating the destiny of a unique genius (down to the jealousy, down to the filth, down to the stab of seeing her almond-shaped eyes turn to blond Cassio behind her peacock-feathered fan) even if one cannot imitate his verse. She liked mine though, and would scarcely have yawned as the other was wont to do every time her husband's poem happened to exceed the length of a sonnet. If she has remained a phantom to me, I may have been one to her: I suppose she had been solely attracted by the obscurity of my poetry; then tore a hole through its veil and saw a stranger's unloveable face.

VLADIMIR NABOKOV

Oxford

TASK 16

Comment on anything you find interesting in one of the following: *Man in Black* by Sylvia Plath (published 1959) and *Ulysses* by James Joyce (1922). Consider, for example, what the passage or poem is about, the impression it makes on you, the means the writer uses to create that impression and convey his or her thought.

(a)   *Man in Black*

Where the three magenta
Breakwaters take the shove
And suck of the grey sea

To the left, and the wave
Unfists against the dun
Barb-wired headland of

The Deer Island prison
With its trim piggeries
Hen Huts and cattle green

To the right, and March ice
Glazes rock pools yet,
Snuff-coloured sand cliffs rise

Over a great stone spit
Bared by each falling tide,
And you, across those white

Stones, strode out in your dead
Black coat, black shoes, and your
Black hair till there you stood,

Fixed vortex on the far
Tip, riveting stones, air
All of it, together.

SYLVIA PLATH

b)   *Ulysses*

Mr Leopold Bloom ate with relish the inner organs of beasts and fowls. He liked thick giblet soup, nutty gizzards, a stuffed roast heart, liver slices fried with crustcrumbs, fried hencod's roes. Most of all he liked grilled mutton kidneys which gave to his palate a fine tang of faintly scented urine.

Kidneys were in his mind as he moved about the kitchen softly, righting her breakfast things on the humpy tray. Gelid light and air were in the kitchen but out of doors gentle summer morning everywhere. Made him feel a bit peckish.

The coals were reddening.

Another slice of bread and butter: three, four: right. She didn't like her plate full. Right. He turned from the tray, lifted the kettle from the hob and set it sideways on the fire. It sat there, dull and squat, its spout stuck out. Cup of tea soon. Good. Mouth dry. The cat walked stiffly round a leg of the table with tail on high.

—'Mrkgnao!'

—'O, there you are,' Mr Bloom said, turning from the fire.

The cat mewed in answer and stalked again stiffly round a leg of table, mewing. Just how she stalks over my writingtable. Prr. Scratch my head. Prr.

Mr Bloom watched curiously, kindly, the lithe black form. Clean to see: the gloss of her sleek hide, the white button under the butt of her tail, the green flashing eyes. He bent down to her, his hands on his knees.

—'Milk for the pussens,' he said.

—'Mrkgnao!' the cat cried.

They call them stupid. They understand what we say better than we understand them. She understands all she wants to. Vindictive too. Cruel. Her nature. Curious mice never squeal. Seem to like it. Wonder what I look like to her. Height of a tower? No, she can jump me.

—'Afraid of the chickens she is,' he said mockingly. 'Afraid of the chookchooks. I never saw such a stupid pussens as the pussens.'

—'Mrkgnao!' the cat said loudly.

JAMES JOYCE

Oxford

TASK 17

Write on either or both of the following passages, from *The Way of all Flesh* by Samuel Butler, and *Advice to a Husband* by William Cobbet (1829). You should draw attention to anything which you find interesting in relation to other nineteenth-century writing that you know.

The following extract is from a novel written between 1872 and 1884. In the extract, the year is 1831, and Theobald, a young vicar, has just married Christina Allaby, a clergyman's daughter, after a five years' engagement.

EXTRACT

(a)   *The Way of all Flesh*

For some time the pair said nothing: what it is they must have felt during the first half hour, the reader must guess, for it is beyond my power to tell him; at the end of that time, however, Theobald had rummaged up a conclusion from some odd corner of his soul to the effect that now he and Christina were married the sooner they fell into their future mutual relations the better. If people who are in any difficulty will only do the first little reasonable thing which they can clearly recognise as reasonable, they will always find the next step more easy both to see and take. What, then, thought Theobald, was here at this moment the first and most obvious matter to be considered, and what would be an equitable view of his and Christina's relative positions in respect to it? Clearly their first dinner was their first joint entry into the duties and pleasures of married life. No less clearly it was Christina's duty to order it, and his to eat it and pay for it.

The arguments leading to this conclusion, and the conclusion itself, flashed upon Theobald about three and a half miles after he had left Crampsford on the road to Newmarket. He had breakfasted early, but his usual appetite had failed him. They had left the vicarage at noon without staying for the wedding breakfast. Theobald liked an early dinner; it dawned upon him that he was beginning to be hungry; from this to the conclusion stated in the preceding paragraph the steps had been easy. After a few minutes' further reflection he broached the matter to his bride, and thus the ice was broken.

Mrs Theobald was not prepared for so sudden an assumption of importance. Her nerves, never of the strongest, had been strung out to their highest tension by the event of the morning. She wanted to escape observation; she was conscious of looking a little older than she quite liked to look as a bride who had been married that morning; she feared the landlady, the chamber-maid, the waiter — everybody and everything; her heart beat so fast that she could hardly speak, much less go through the ordeal of ordering dinner in a strange hotel with a strange landlady. She begged and prayed to be let off. If Theobald would only order dinner this once, she would order it any day and every day in future.

But the inexorable Theobald was not to be put off with such absurd excuses. He was master now. Had not Christina less than two hours ago promised solemnly to honour and obey him, and was she turning restive over such a trifle as this? The loving smile departed from his face, and was succeeded by a scowl which that old Turk, his father, might have envied. 'Stuff and nonsense, my dearest Christina,' he exclaimed mildly, and stamped his foot upon the floor of the carriage. 'It's a wife's duty to order her husband's dinner; you are my wife, and I shall expect you to order mine.' For Theobald was nothing if he was not logical.

The bride began to cry, and said that he was unkind; whereon he said nothing, but revolved unutterable things in his heart. Was this, then, the end of his six years of unflagging devotion? Was it for this that, when Christina had offered to let him off, he had stuck to his engagement? Was this the outcome of her talks about duty and spiritual mindedness — that now upon the very day of her marriage she should fail to see that the first step in obedience to God lay in obedience to himself? He would drive back to Crampsford; he would complain to Mr and Mrs Allaby; he didn't mean to have married Christina; he hadn't married her; it was all a hideous dream; he would — But a voice kept ringing in his ears which said: 'You CAN'T, CAN'T, CAN'T.'

'CAN'T I?' screamed the unhappy creature to himself.

'No,' said the remorseless voice, 'YOU CAN'T. YOU ARE A MARRIED MAN.'

SAMUEL BUTLER

This extract is taken from one of a series of articles giving advice to young men at various stages of their lives.

(b) *Advice to a Husband*

A husband thus under command is the most contemptible of God's creatures. Nobody can place reliance on him for anything; whether in the capacity of employer or employed, you are never sure of him. No bargain is firm, no engagement sacred, with such a man. Feeble as a reed before the boisterous she-commander, he is bold in injustice towards those whom it pleases her caprice to mark out for vengeance. In the eyes of neighbours, for friends such a man cannot have, in the eyes of servants, in the eyes even of the beggars at the door, such a man is a mean and despicable creature, though he may roll in wealth and possess great talents into the bargain. Such a man has, in fact, no property; he has nothing that he can rightly call his own; he is a beggarly dependent under his own roof; and if he have anything of the man left in him, and if there be a rope or river near, the sooner he betakes himself to the one or the other the better. How many men, how many families, have I known brought to utter ruin by the husband suffering himself to be subdued, to be cowed down, to be held in fear, of even a virtuous wife! What, then, must be the lot of him who submits to a commander who, at the same time, sets all virtue at defiance!

Women are a sisterhood. They make common cause on behalf of the sex; and, indeed, this is natural enough, when we consider the vast power the law gives us over them. The law is for us, and they combine, wherever they can, to mitigate its effects. This is perfectly natural, and, to a certain extent, laudable, evincing fellow-feeling and public spirit; but when carried to the length of 'he sha'n't', it is despotism on the one side, and slavery on the other. Watch, therefore, the incipient steps of encroachment; they come on so slowly, so softly, that you must be sharp-sighted if you perceive them, put at once an effectual stop to their progress. Never mind the pain that it may give you: a day of pain at this time will spare you years of pain in time to come. Many a man has been made miserable, and made his wife miserable too, for a score or two of years, only for want of resolution to bear one day of pain: and it is a great deal to bear; it is a great deal to do to thwart the desire of one whom you so dearly love, and whose virtues daily render her more and more dear to you. But (and this is one of the most admirable of the mother's traits) as she herself will, while the tears stream from her eyes, force the nauseous medicine down the throat of her child, whose every cry is a dagger to her heart; as she herself has the courage to do this for the sake of her child, why should you flinch from the performance of a still more important and more sacred duty towards herself, as well as towards you and your children?

Am I recommending tyranny? Am I recommending disregard of the wife's opinions and wishes? Am I recommending a reserve towards her that would seem to say that she was not trustworthy, or not a party interested in her husband's affairs? By no means: on the contrary, though I would keep anything disagreeable from her, I should not enjoy the prospect of good without making her a participator. But reason says, and God has said, that it is the duty of wives to be obedient to their husbands; and the very nature of things prescribes that there must be a head of every house, and an undivided authority. And then it is so clearly just that the authority should rest with him on whose head rests the whole responsibility, that a woman, when patiently reasoned with on the subject, must be a virago in her very nature not to submit with docility to the terms of her marriage vow.

WILLIAM COBBETT
Oxford

TASK 18

The following passages, *Essay XVII — of Travel* by France Bacon (1597) and *Autobiography* by Edward Gibbon (1796) are concerned with travel. Choosing one or both of them, give an account of anything in content or expression which reflects the literature of the period which you have studied.

EXTRACT

(a)

Essay XVII — of Travel

Travel, in the younger sort, is a part of education; in the elder, a part of experience. He that travelleth into a country before he hath some entrance into the language, goeth to school, and not travel. That young men travel under some tutor, or grave servant, I allow well; so that he be such a one that hath the language and hath been in the country before; whereby he may be able to tell them what things are worthy to be seen in the country where they go; what acquaintances they are to seek; what exercises or discipline the place yieldeth. For else young men shall go hooded, and look abroad little. It is a strange thing that in sea-voyages, where there is nothing to be seen but sea and sky, men should make diaries, but in land-travel, wherein so much is to be observed, for the most part they omit it; as if chance were fitter to be registered than observation. Let diaries, therefore, be brought in use. The things to be seen and observed are: the courts of princes, specially when they give audience to ambassadors; the courts of justice, while they sit and hear causes, and so of consistories ecclesiastic; the churches and monasteries, with the monuments which are therin extant; the walls and fortifications of cities and towns, and so havens and harbours; antiquities and ruins; libraries; colleges, disputations, and lectures, where any are; shipping and navies; houses and gardens of state and pleasure, near great cities; armouries; arsenals; magazines; exchanges; burses; warehouses; exercises of horsemanship, fencing, training of soldiers, and the like; comedies, such whereunto the better sort of persons do resort; treasuries of jewels and robes; cabinets and rarities; and, to conclude, whatsoever is memorable in the places where they go. After all which the tutors or servants ought to make diligent enquiry. As for triumphs, masques, feasts, weddings, funerals, capital executions, and such shews, men need not be put in mind of them; yet they are not to be neglected.

FRANCIS BACON

(b)   *Autobiography*

My temper is not very susceptible of enthusiasm, and the enthusiasm which I do not feel I ever scorned to affect. But, at the distance of twenty-five years, I can neither forget nor express the strong emotions which agitated my mind as I first approached and entered the eternal city. After a sleepless night, I trod, with lofty step, the ruins of the Forum; each memorable spot where Romulus stood, or Tully spoke, or Caesar fell, was at once present to my eye; and several days of intoxication were lost or enjoyed before I could descend to a cool and minute investigation. My guide was Mr Byers, a Scotch antiquary of experience and taste; but, in the daily labour of eighteen weeks, the powers of attention were sometimes fatigued, till I was myself qualified, in a last review, to select and study the capital works of ancient and modern art. Six weeks were borrowed for my tour of Naples, the most populous of cities, relative to size, whose luxurious inhabitants seem to dwell on the confines of paradise and hell-fire. I was presented to the boy-king by our new envoy, Sir William Hamilton; who, wisely diverting his correspondence from the Secretary of State to the Royal Society and British Museum, has elucidated a country of such inestimable value to the naturalist and antiquarian. On my return, I fondly embraced, for the last time, the miracles of ancient Rome; but I departed without kissing the foot of Rezzonico (Clement XIII), who neither possessed the wit of his predecessor Lambertini, nor the virtues of his successor Ganganelli. In my pilgrimage from Rome to Loretto I again crossed the Apennine; from the coast of the Adriatic I traversed a fruitful and populous country, which could alone disprove the paradox of Montesquieu, that modern Italy is a desert. Without adopting the exclusive prejudice of the natives, I sincerely admire the paintings of the Bologna school. I hastened to escape from the sad solitude of Ferrara, which in the age of Caesar was still more desolate. The spectacle of Venice afforded some hours of astonishment; the University of Padua is a dying taper; but Verona still boasts her amphitheatre; and his native Vicenza is adorned by the classic architecture of Palladio: the road of Lombardy and Piedmont (did Montesquieu find them without inhabitants?) led me back to Milan, Turin, and the passage of Mount Cenis, where I again crossed the Alps in my way to Lyons.

The use of foreign travel has been often debated as a general question; but the conclusion must be finally applied to the character and circumstances of the individual. With the education of boys, *where* or *how* they may pass over some juvenile years with the least mischief to themselves or others, I have no concern. But after supposing the previous and indispensable requisites of age, judgement, a competent knowledge of men and books, and a freedom from domestic prejudices, I will briefly describe the qualifications which I deem most essential to a traveller. He should be endowed with an active, indefatigable vigour of mind and body, which can seize every mode of conveyance, and support, with a careless smile, every hardship of the road, the weather, or the inn. The benefits of foreign travel will correspond with the degrees of these qualifications; but, in this sketch, those to whom I am known will not accuse me of framing my own panegyric. It was at Rome, on the 15th of October, 1764, as I sat musing amidst the ruins of the Capitol, while all the barefooted friars were singing vespers in the Temple of Jupiter, that the idea of writing the decline and fall of the city first started to my mind. But my original plan was circumscribed to the decay of the city rather than of the empire: and, though reading and reflections began to point towards that object, some years elapsed, and several avocations intervened, before I was seriously engaged in the execution of that laborious work.

EDWARD GIBBON

Oxford

TASK 19

The passages below are conclusions to three novels: *The Rainbow* by D H Lawrence (1915), *Howards End* by E M Forster (1910) and *Vanity Fair* by W M Thackeray (1848).

Questions

(a) These writers conclude their novels in different ways. What, in your view, is each most concerned to do in these last paragraphs? You may refer to two or all three in your answer.

(b) 'In these conclusions, several characters alienate us' (Chartour). Give your comments on this judgement.

(c) Doom — gloom — hope. How do these novels end?

EXTRACT

(a)

The Rainbow

Strange, what a void separated him and her. She liked him now, as she liked a memory, some bygone self. He was something of the past, finite. He was that which is known. She felt a poignant affection for him, as for that which is past. But, when she looked with her face forward, he was not. Nay, when she looked ahead, into the undiscovered land before her, what was there she could recognise but a fresh glow of light and inscrutable trees going up from the earth like smoke. It was the unknown, the unexplored, the undiscovered upon whose shore she had landed, alone, after crossing the void, the darkness which washed the New World and the Old.

There would be no child: she was glad. If there had been a child, it would have made little difference, however. She would have kept the child and herself, she would not have gone to Skrebensky. Anton belonged to the past.

There came the cablegram from Skrebensky: 'I am married.' An old pain and anger and contempt stirred in her. Did he belong so utterly to the cast-off past? She repudiated him. He was as he was. It was good that he was as he was. Who was she to have a man according to her own desire? It was not for her to create, but to recognise a man created by God. The man should come from the Infinite and she should hail him. She was glad she could not create her man. She was glad she had nothing to do with his creation. She was glad that this lay within the scope of that vaster power in which she rested at last. The man would come out of Eternity to which she herself belonged.

As she grew better, she sat to watch a new creation. As she sat at her window, she saw the people go by in the street below, colliers, women, children, walking each in the husk of an old fruition, but visible through the husk, the swelling and the heaving contour of the new germination. In the still, silenced forms of the colliers she saw a sort of suspense, a waiting in pain for the new liberation; she saw the same in the false hard confidence of the women. The confidence of the women was brittle. It would break quickly to reveal the strength and patient effort of the new germination.

In everything she saw she grasped and groped to find the creation of the living God, instead of the old, hard barren form of bygone living. Sometimes great terror possessed her. Sometimes she lost touch, she lost her feeling, she could only know the old horror of the husk which bound in her and all mankind. They were all in prison, they were all going mad.

She saw in the stiffened bodies of the colliers, which seemed already enclosed in a coffin, she saw their unchanging eyes, the eyes of those who are buried alive: she saw the hard, cutting edges of the new houses, which seemed to spread over the hillside in their insentient triumph, a triumph of horrible, amorphous angles and straight lines, the expression of corruption, triumphant and unopposed, corruption so pure that it is hard and brittle: she saw the dun atmosphere over the blackened hills opposite, the dark blotches of houses, slate roofed and amorphous, the old church-tower standing up in hideous obsoleteness above raw new houses on the crest of the hill, the amorphous, brittle, hard edged new houses advancing from Beldover to meet the corrupt new houses from Lethley, the houses of Lethley advancing to mix with the houses of Hainor, a dry, brittle, terrible corruption spreading over the face of the land, and she was sick with a nausea so deep that she perished as she sat. And then, in the blowing clouds, she saw a band of faint iridescence colouring in faint colours a portion of the hill. And forgetting, startled, she looked for the hovering colour and saw a rainbow forming itself. In one place it gleamed fiercely, and, her heart anguished with hope, she sought the shadow of iris where the bow should be. Steadily the colour gathered, mysteriously, from nowhere, it took presence upon itself, there was a faint, vast rainbow. The arc bended and strengthened itself till it arched indomitable, making great architecture of light and colour and the space of heaven, its pedestals luminous in the corruption of new houses on the low hill, its arch the top of heaven.

And the rainbow stood on the earth. She knew that the sordid people who crept hard-scaled and separate on the face of the world's corruption were living still, that the rainbow was arched in their blood and would quiver to life in their spirit, that they would cast off their horny covering of disintegration, that new, clean, naked bodies would issue to a new generation, to a new growth, rising to the light and the wind and the clean rain of heaven. She saw in the rainbow the earth's new architecture, the old brittle corruption of houses and factories swept away, the world built up in a living fabric of Truth, fitting to the over-arching heaven.

D H LAWRENCE

(b)   *Howards End*   EXTRACT

Clumsy of movement — for he had spent all his life in the saddle — Paul drove his foot against the paint of the front door. Mrs Wilcox gave a little cry of annoyance. She did not like anything scratched. She stopped in the hall to take Dolly's bow and gloves out of a vase.

Her husband was lying in a great leather chair in the dining-room, and by his side, holding his hand rather ostentatiously, was Evie. Dolly, dressed in purple, sat near the window. The room was a little dark and airless; they were obliged to keep it like this until the carting of the hay. Margaret joined the family without speaking; the five of them had already met at tea, and she knew quite well what was going to be said. Averse to wasting her time, she went on sewing. The clock struck six.

'Is this going to suit everyone?' said Henry in a weary voice. He used the old phrases, but their effect was unexpected and shadowy. 'Because I don't want you all coming here later and complaining that I have been unfair.'

'It is apparently going to suit us,' said Paul.

'I beg your pardon, my boy. You have only to speak, and I will leave the house to you instead.'

Paul frowned ill-temperedly, and began scratching at his arm. 'As I've given up the outdoor life that suited me, and I have come home to look after the business, it's no good my settling down here,' he said at last. 'It's not really the country, and it's not the town.'

'Very well. Does my arrangement suit you, Evie?'

'Of course, father.'

'And you, Dolly?'

Dolly raised her faded little face, which sorrow could wither but not steady. 'Perfectly splendidly,' she said. 'I thought Charles wanted it for the boys, but last time I saw him he said no, because we cannot possibly live in this part of England again. Charles says we ought to change our name, but I can't think what to, for Wilcox just suits Charles and me, and I can't think of any other name.'

There was a general silence. Dolly looked nervously round, fearing that she had been inappropriate. Paul continued to scratch his arm.

'Then I leave Howards End to my wife absolutely,' said Henry. 'And let everyone understand that; and after I am dead let there be no jealousy and no surprise.'

Margaret did not answer. There was something uncanny in her triumph. She, who had never expected to conquer anyone, had charged straight through these Wilcoxes and broken up their lives.

'In consequence, I leave my wife no money,' said Henry. 'That is her own wish. All that she would have had will be divided among you. I am also giving you a great deal in my lifetime, so that you may be independent of me. That is her wish, too. She is also giving away a great deal of money. She intends to diminish her income by half during the next ten years; she intends when she dies to leave the house to her — to her nephew, down in the field. Is all that clear? Does everyone understand?'

Paul rose to his feet. He was accustomed to natives, and a very little shook him out of the Englishman. Feeling manly and cynical, he said: 'Down in the field? Oh, come! I think we might have had the whole establishment, piccaninnies included.'

Mrs Cahill whispered: 'Don't, Paul. You promised you'd take care.' Feeling a woman of the world, she rose and prepared to take her leave.

Her father kissed her. 'Good-bye, old girl,' he said; 'don't you worry about me.'

'Good-bye, dad.'

Then it was Dolly's turn. Anxious to contribute, she laughed nervously, and said: 'Good-bye, Mr Wilcox. It does seem curious that Mrs Wilcox should have left Margaret Howards End, and yet she get it, after all.'

From Evie came a sharply-drawn breath. 'Good-bye,' she said to Margaret, and kissed her.

And again and again fell the word, like the ebb of a dying sea.

'Good-bye.'

'Good-bye, Dolly.'

'So long, father.'

'Good-bye, my boy; always take care of yourself.'

'Good-bye, Mrs Wilcox.'

'Good-bye.'

Margaret saw their visitors to the gate. Then she returned to her husband and laid her head on his hands. He was pitiably tired. But Dolly's remark had interested her. At last she said: 'Could you tell me, Henry, what was that about Mrs Wilcox having left me Howards End?'

Tranquilly he replied: 'Yes, she did. But that is a very old story. When she was ill and you were so kind to her she wanted to make you some return, and, not being herself at the time, scribbled 'Howards End' on a piece of paper. I went into it thoroughly, and, as it was clearly fanciful, I set it aside, little knowing what my Margaret would be to me in the future.'

Margaret was silent. Something shook her life in its inmost recesses, and she shivered.

'I didn't do wrong, did I?' he asked, bending down.

'You didn't, darling. Nothing has been done wrong.'

From the garden came laughter. 'Here they are at last!' exclaimed Henry, disengaging himself with a smile. Helen rushed into the gloom, holding Tom by one hand and carrying her baby on the other. There were shouts of infectious joy.

'The field's cut!' Helen cried excitedly — 'the big meadow! We've seen to the very end, and it'll be such a crop of hay as never!'

E M FORSTER

(c) *Vanity Fair*

She was never Lady Crawley, though she continued so to call herself. His Excellency, Colonel Rawdon Crawley died of yellow fever at Coventry Island, most deeply loved and deplored, and six weeks before the demise of his brother, Sir Pitt. The estate consequently devolved upon the present Sir Rawdon Crawley, Bart.

He, too, has declined to see his mother, to whom he makes a liberal allowance, and who, besides, appears to be very wealthy. The Baronet lives entirely at Queen's Crawley, with Lady Jane and her daughter; whilst Rebecca, Lady Crawley, chiefly hangs about in Bath and Cheltenham, where a very strong party of excellent people consider her to be a most injured woman. She has her enemies. Who has not? Her life is her answer to them. She busies herself in works of piety. She goes to church, and never without a footman. Her name is in all the Charity Lists. The Destitute Orangegirl, the Neglected Washerwoman, the Distressed Muffinman, find in her a fast and generous friend. She is always having stalls at Fancy Fairs for the benefit of these hapless beings. Emmy, her children, and the Colonel, coming to London some time back, found themselves suddenly before her at one of these fairs. She cast her eyes down demurely and smiled as they started away from her; Emmy skurrying off on the arm of George (now grown a dashing young gentleman), and the Colonel seizing up his little Janey, of whom he is fonder than anything in the world — fonder even than of his 'History of the Punjaub.'

'Fonder than he is of me,' Emmy thinks, with a sigh. But he never said a word to Amelia that was not kind and gentle, or thought of a want of hers that he did not try to gratify.

Ah! *Vanitas Vanitatum*! Which of us is happy in this world? Which of us has his desire? or, having it, is satisfied? — Come, children, let us shut up the box and the puppets, for our play is played out.

W M THACKERAY
NEAB

The following extracts are from two modern plays — *The Caretaker* by Harold Pinter (1960) and *Waiting for Godot* by Samuel Beckett (1954).

Questions

(a) Comment in as much detail as you can about the way in which each writer treats the wearing of shoes.

(b) Both playwrights in these extracts choose to present dialogue between two people. Compare the ways in which this dramatic form is handled by each playwright.

(c) Perhaps the conversations seem trivial to you. Are there any places in either of the extracts where you sense deeper notes are sounded? If so, explain where and how.

(a) *The Caretaker*

ASTON: What happened when you got there, then?

> *Pause.*

DAVIES: I used to know a bootmaker in Acton. He was a good mate to me.
You know what that bastard monk said to me?

> *Pause.*

How many more Blacks you got around here then?
ASTON: What?
DAVIES: You got any more Blacks around here?
ASTON (*holding out the shoes*): See if these are any good.

DAVIES: You know what that bastard monk said to me? (*He looks over to the shoes.*) I think those'd be a bit small.

ASTON: Would they?

DAVIES: No, don't look the right size.

ASTON: Not bad trim.

DAVIES: Can't wear shoes that don't fit. Nothing worse. I said to this monk, here, I said, look here, mister, he opened the door, big door, he opened it, look here mister, I said, I come all the way down here, look, I said, I showed him these, I said, you haven't got a pair of shoes, have you, a pair of shoes, I said, enough to keep me on my way. Look at these, they're nearly out, I said, they're no good to me. I heard you got a stock of shoes here. Piss off, he said to me. Now look here, I said, I'm an old man, you can't talk to me like that, I don't care who you are. If you don't piss off, he says, I'll kick you all the way to the gate. Now look here, I said, now wait a minute, all I'm asking for is a pair of shoes, you don't want to start taking liberties with me, it's taken me three days to get here, I said to him, three days without a bite, I'm worth a bite to eat, en I? Get out round the corner to the kitchen, he says, get out round the corner, and when you've had your meal, piss off out of it. I went round to this kitchen, see? Meal they give me! A bird, I tell you, a little tiny bird, he could have ate it in under two minutes. Right, they said to me, you've had your meal, get off out of it. Meal? I said, what do you think I am, a dog? Nothing better than a dog. What do you think I am, a wild animal? What about them shoes I come all the way here to get I heard you was giving away? I've got a good mind to report you to your mother superior. One of them, an Irish hooligan, come at me. I cleared out. I took a short cut to Watford and picked up a pair there. Got onto the North Circular, just past Hendon, the sole came off, right where I was walking. Lucky I had my old ones wrapped up, still carrying them, otherwise I'd have been finished, man. So I've had to stay with these, you see, they're gone, they're no good, all the good's gone out of them.

ASTON: Try these.

DAVIES *takes the shoes, takes off his sandals and tries them on.*

DAVIES: Not a bad pair of shoes. (*He trudges round the room.*) They're strong, all right. Yes. Not a bad shape of shoe. This leather's hardy, en't? Very hardy. Some bloke tried to flog me some suede the other day. I wouldn't wear them. Can't beat leather, for wear. Suede goes off, it creases, it stains for life in five minutes. You can't beat leather. Yes. Good shoe this.

ASTON: Good.

Davies waggles his feet.

DAVIES: Don't fit though.

ASTON: Oh?

DAVIES: No, I got a very broad foot.

ASTON: Mmnn.

DAVIES: These are too pointed, you see.

ASTON: Ah.

DAVIES: They'd cripple me in a week. I mean these ones I got on, they're no good but at least they're comfortable. Not much cop, but I mean they don't hurt. (*He takes them off and gives them back.*) Thanks anyway, mister.

ASTON: I'll see what I can look out for you.

DAVIES: Good luck. I can't go on like this. Can't get from one place to another. And I'll have to be moving about, you see, trying to get fixed up.

ASTON: Where are you going to go?

DAVIES: Oh, I've got one or two things in mind. I'm waiting for the weather to break.

Pause.

ASTON (*attending to the toaster*): Would . . . would you like to sleep here?

DAVIES: Here?

ASTON: You can sleep here if you like.

DAVIES: Here? Oh, I don't know about that.

Pause.

How long for?

ASTON: Till you . . . get yourself fixed up.

DAVIES (*sitting*): Ay well, that . . .

ASTON: Get yourself sorted out . . .

DAVIES: Oh, I'll be fixed up . . . pretty soon now . . .

Pause.

Where would I sleep?

ASTON: Here. The other rooms would . . . would be no good to you.

DAVIES (*rising, looking about*): Here? Where?

ASTON (*rising, pointing upstage right*): There's a bed behind all that.

DAVIES: Oh, I see. Well, that's handy. Well, that's . . . I tell you what, I might do that . . . just till I get myself sorted out. You got enough furniture here.

ASTON: I picked it up. Just keeping it here for the time being. Thought it might come in handy.

DAVIES: This gas stove work, do it?

ASTON: No.

DAVIES: What do you do for your cup of tea?

ASTON: Nothing.

DAVIES: That's a bit rough. (*Davies observes the planks.*) You building something?

ASTON: I might be building a shed out the back.

DAVIES: Carpenter, eh? (*He turns to the lawn-mower.*) Got a lawn.

ASTON: Have a look.

HAROLD PINTER

(b) ### Waiting for Godot

EXTRACT

Estragon, sitting on a low mound, is trying to take off his boot. He pulls at it with both hands, panting. He gives up, exhausted, rests, tries again. As before.

Enter VLADIMIR.

ESTRAGON (*giving up again*): Nothing to be done.

VLADIMIR (*advancing with short, stiff strides, legs wide apart*): I'm beginning to come round to that opinion. All my life I've tried to put it from me, saying, Vladimir, be reasonable, you haven't tried everything. And I resumed the struggle. (*He broods, musing on the struggle. Turning to Estragon.*) So there you are again.

ESTRAGON: Am I?

VLADIMIR: I'm glad to see you back. I thought you were gone for ever.

ESTRAGON: Me too.

VLADIMIR: Together again at last! We'll have to celebrate this. But how? (*He reflects.*) Get up till I embrace you.

ESTRAGON (*irritably*): Not now, not now.

VLADIMIR (*hurt, coldly*): May one enquire where His Highness spent the night?

ESTRAGON: In a ditch.

VLADIMIR (*admiringly*): A ditch! Where?

ESTRAGON (*without gesture*): Over there.

VLADIMIR: And they didn't beat you?

ESTRAGON: Beat me? Certainly they beat me.

VLADIMIR: The same lot as usual?

ESTRAGON: The same? I don't know.

VLADIMIR: When I think of it . . . all these years . . . but for me . . . where would you be . . . ? (*Decisively.*) You'd be nothing more than a little heap of bones at the present minute, no doubt about it.

ESTRAGON: And what of it?

VLADIMIR (*gloomily*): It's too much for one man. (*Pause. Cheerfully.*) On the other hand what's the good of losing heart now, that's what I say. We should have thought of it a million years ago, in the nineties.

ESTRAGON: Ah, stop blathering and help me off with this bloody thing.

VLADIMIR: Hand in hand from the top of the Eiffel Tower, among the first. We were presentable in those days. Now it's too late. They wouldn't even let us up. (*Estragon tears at his boot.*) What are you doing?

ESTRAGON: Taking off my boot. Did that never happen to you?

VLADIMIR: Boots must be taken off every day, I'm tired of telling you that. Why don't you listen to me?

ESTRAGON (*feebly*): Help me!

VLADIMIR: It hurts?

ESTRAGON: Hurts! He wants to know if it hurts!

VLADIMIR (*angrily*): No one ever suffers but you. I don't count. I'd like to hear what you'd say if you had what I have.

ESTRAGON: It hurts?

VLADIMIR: Hurts! He wants to know if it hurts!

ESTRAGON (*pointing*): You might button it all the same.

VLADIMIR (*stooping*): True. (*He buttons his fly.*) Never neglect the little things of life.

ESTRAGON: What do you expect, you always wait till the last moment.

VLADIMIR (*musingly*): The last moment . . . (*He meditates.*) Hope deferred maketh the something sick, who said that?

ESTRAGON: Why don't you help me?

VLADIMIR: Sometimes I feel it coming all the same. Then I go all queer. (*He takes off his hat, peers inside it, feels about inside it, shakes it, puts it on again.*) How shall I say? Relieved and at the same time (*he searches for the word*) . . . appalled. (*With emphasis.*) A P – P A L L E D. (*He takes off his hat again, peers inside it.*) Funny. (*He knocks on the crown as though to dislodge a foreign body, peers inside it again, puts it on again.*) Nothing to be done. (*Estragon with a supreme effort succeeds in pulling off his boot. He looks inside it, feels about inside it, turns it upside down, shakes it, looks on the ground to see if anything has fallen out, finds nothing, feels inside it again, staring sightlessly before him.*) Well?

ESTRAGON: Nothing.

VLADIMIR: Show.

ESTRAGON: There's nothing to show.

VLADIMIR: Try and put it on again.

ESTRAGON (*examining his foot*): I'll air it for a bit.

VLADIMIR: There's man all over for you, blaming on his boots the faults of his feet. (*He takes off his hat again, peers inside it, feels about inside it, knocks on the crown, blows into it, puts it on again.*) This is getting alarming. (*Silence. Vladimir deep in thought. Estragon pulling at his toes.*) One of the thieves was saved. (*Pause.*) It's a reasonable percentage. (*Pause.*) Gogo.

ESTRAGON: What?

VLADIMIR: Suppose we repented?

ESTRAGON: Repented what?

VLADIMIR: Oh . . . (*He reflects.*) We wouldn't have to go into the details.

ESTRAGON: Our being born?

Vladimir breaks into a hearty laugh which he immediately stifles, his hand pressed to his pubis, his face contorted.

VLADIMIR: One daren't laugh any more.

ESTRAGON: Dreadful privation.

VLADIMIR: Merely smile. (*He smiles suddenly from ear to ear, keeps smiling, ceases as suddenly.*) It's not the same thing. Nothing to be done.

SAMUEL BECKETT

NEAB

By a close study of the following poem, *Red Hills of Home*, by the Zimbabwean poet Chenjcrai Hove, consider how effectively the poet's protest is communicated to the reader.

Red Hills of Home

Father grew up here
tuning his heart
to the sound of the owl from the moist green hills
beyond, the eagle swam in the air
while mother-ant dragged an unknown victim to a known hole printed on the
familiar receding earth.

I grew up here
father died underground seven rainless seasons ago
and the burial news was all we had to bury.
Now the featherless eagle like roast meat,
recites the misery of the dusty sky.
Mother-ant never surfaces
for father is enough meat, underground.
The green hills of home died,
Red hills cut the sky
and the nearby sooty homes of peasants
live under the roaring bulldozer.
Yesterday Sabhuku Manyonga had the push
of muscular hands on his chest
and now lives in drunken exile.

Red hills have come
with wounds whose pus
suffocates the peasant.
The peasant's baby sleeps
knowing only thin dreams of moonlight joy.
Dying too are the songs
of the seasons that father once sang.
Red hills and the smoke of man-made thunder
plunder the land under contact.
If father rose from the dead
he would surely not know
the very ant-hill embracing his blood
buried with the umbilical cord.
Here, on this bit of ground
earth once lay pregnant
but now
the sacred hill bleeds
robbed even of her decent name,
her holy cows are milked
by hunger-laden hands
whose mouths eat man

gulped down by this eerie giant's throat
sitting where you once flowed
with calm holy water.

Red hills and the smell of exile;
Chipo died this morning
no more burial song ripped the air
nor do we feel safe to bury her
knowing tomorrow a bulldozer
comes to scatter these malnourished bones.
Red hills and the smell of exile.
Exile breathing over our shoulder
in a race that already looks desperate.
Red hills, and the pulse of exile
telling us that this is home no more.

CHENJERAI HOVE

UCLES

TASK 22

Analyse the language and the dramatic effectiveness of this scene from *Bartholomew Fair* by Ben Jonson (1614). It is the opening of Act 2, where the fair, which is central to the play, begins to come to life.

EXTRACT

Bartholomew Fair

The Fair.

Enter LANTERN LEATHERHEAD, JOAN TRASH, *and the people of the Fair; they begin to erect their booths and stalls.*

Enter JUSTICE OVERDO, *alone, disguised as a madman.*

OVERDO (*aside*): Well, in Justice' name, and the King's, and for the Commonwealth! Defy all the world, Adam Overdo, for a disguise, and all story; for thou hast fitted thyself, I swear. Fain would I meet with Lynceus now, that eagle's eye, that piercing Epidaurian servant (as my Quintas Horace calls him), that could discover a Justice of Peace (and lately of the quorum) under this covering. They may have seen many a fool in the habit of a Justice; but never till now a Justice in the habit of a fool. Thus must we do, though, that wake for public good; and thus hath the wise magistrate done in all ages. There is a doing of right out of wrong, if the way be found. Never shall I enough commend a worthy worshipful man, sometime a capital member of this City, for his high wisdom in this point, who would take you, now the habit of a porter, now of a carman, now of the dog-killer, in this month of August; and in the winter a seller of tinder-boxes. And what would he do in all these shapes? Marry, go you into every ale-house, and down into every cellar; measure the length of puddings, take the gauge of black pots and cans, ay, and custards, with a stick; and their circumference, with a thread; weigh the loaves of bread on his middle-finger; then would he send for 'em, home; give the puddings to the poor, the bread to the hungry, the custards to his children; break the pots and burn the cans himself; he would not trust his corrupt officers; he would do't himself. Would all men in authority would follow this worthy precedent! For, alas, as we are public persons, what do we know? Nay, what can we know? We hear with other men's ears; we see with other men's eyes. A foolish constable or a sleepy watchman is all our information; he slanders a gentleman by the virtue of his place, as he calls it, and we, by the vice of ours, must believe him. As, a while gone, they made me, yea me, to mistake an honest zealous pursuivant for a seminary, and a proper young Bachelor of Music for a bawd. This we are subject to, that live in a high place; all our intelligence is idle, and most of our intelligencers knaves; and, by your leave, ourselves thought little better, if not arrant fools, for believing 'em. I, Adam Overdo, am resolved therefore to make mine own discoveries. Many are the yearly enormities of this Fair, in whose courts of Pie-powders I have the honour during the three days sometimes to sit as a judge. But this is a special day for the detection of those foresaid enormities. Here is my black book for the purpose; this the cloud that hides me; under this covert I shall see and not be seen. Oh, Junius Brutus! And as I begin so I'll end: in Justice' name, and the King's; and for the Commonwealth!

LEATHERHEAD: The Fair's pestilence-dead, methinks; people come not abroad today, whatever the matter is. Do you hear, Sister Trash, Lady o' the Basket? Sit farther with your ginger-bread-progeny there, and hinder not the prospect of my shop, or I'll ha' it proclaimed i' the Fair what stuff they are made on.

TRASH: Why, what stuff are they made on, Brother Leatherhead? Nothing but what's wholesome, I assure you.

LEATHERHEAD: Yes, stale bread, rotten eggs, musty ginger, and dead honey, you know.

OVERDO (*aside*): Ay! have I met with enormity so soon?

LEATHERHEAD: I shall mar your market, old Joan.

TRASH: Mar my market, thou too-proud pedlar? Do thy worst; I defy thee, I, and thy stable of hobby-horses. I pay for my ground as well as thou dost; an' thou wrong'st me, for all thou art parcel-poet and inginer, I'll find a friend shall right me and make a ballad of thee and thy cattel all over. Are you puffed up with the pride of your wares? Your arsedine?

LEATHERHEAD: Go to, old Joan, I'll talk with you anon; and take you down too afore Justice Overdo; he is the man must charm you. I'll ha' you i' the Pie-powders.

TRASH: Charm me? I'll meet thee face to face afore his worship when thou dar'st; and though I be a little crooked o' my body, I'll be found as upright in my dealing as any woman in Smithfield. Charm me?

OVERDO (*aside*): I am glad to hear my name is their terror, yet; this is doing of justice.

Enter PASSENGERS.

LEATHERHEAD: What do you lack? What is't you buy? What do you lack? Rattles, drums, halberts, horses, babies o' the best? Fiddles o' the finest?

Enter COSTER-MONGER (*and* NIGHTINGALE).

COSTER-MONGER: Buy any pears, pears, pears, very fine pears!

TRASH: Buy any gingerbread, gilt gingerbread!

NIGHTINGALE: Hey, now the Fair's a-filling!
   O for a tune to startle
   The birds o' the booths here billing
   Yearly with old Saint Bartle!
   The drunkards are wading,
   The punks and chapmen trading;
   Who'd see the Fair without this lading?
   Buy any ballads; new ballads?

BEN JONSON

TASK 23

Write a detailed analysis of the opening of Act 1 of *Next Time I'll Sing to You* by James Saunders (published 1962).

EXTRACT

Next Time I'll Sing to You

The lights go out. In the darkness MEFF *is heard making his entrance. There is the sound of a collision, a muffled curse, the sound of falling papers, and after a moment* MEFF *is revealed by the light of the match he has struck, crawling on the floor, gathering up the manuscript sheets he has dropped. The lights go up;* MEFF's *match burns his fingers and he shakes it out. He looks up, sorts through the papers until he finds page one, sits on the edge of the platform and starts to read it.*

MEFF: 'There is pretence, and there is the pretence behind pretence. Though the ages of the groping of man from the dark chaos of his beginnings when shrouded by ignorance of his ignorance he stared first blankly at a sky devoid yet even of mystery and clawed himself awkwardly and for reasons unknown to stand steadily on his two back feet —

He stands.

'— to this point in time when falsely secure in the perennial delusion of having reached the point of culmination beyond which stretches the smooth free-coasting slope to perfection of knowledge, perfection of behaviour, perfection of environment he balances upright with such apparent ease as to be able to call his front paws hands . . .

He frowns and glances back to the beginning of the speech.

'— much has been gained —

He searches for the second page, finds it, and continues.

'— and lost. Gained — experience, know how, intellectual dexterity. Lost, simplicity. Lost the understanding beneath understanding, lost the ability to pretend without pretending not to pretend . . .' Godstruth. A man with a wooden leg was walking down the road on his hands until he met a man with a wooden arm walking on his feet. Tell me, said the first man, why do you walk like that? Well, said the second, if I walked on the other it might drop off.' There was an Englishman, an Irishman and a poltergeist, and they bet each other they couldn't do what the other could do. So they went away and three days later they came back. Well? said the Englishman. It's no good, said the Oirishman, The divil Oi could even get me hat off. You're lucky, said the poltergeist, The devil I could!

DUST *has entered. He stands watching* MEFF.

A man walked into a doctor's surgery carrying an enormous plate of jellied eels. Look here, said the receptionist, you can't bring animals in here. Why not, said the man, I've got 'em on a lead.

DUST: *Is this relevant?*

MEFF: Just warming them up. Good audience tonight. They're with us. Laughing like coffins. A one-eyed apothecary was driving a herd of Bacterian camels down Shaftesbury Avenue —

DUST: Do you realize we have rather a lot to go through?

MEFF: Camels?

DUST: When a job's to be done I believe in getting down to it. State your objectives, define your terms of reference, marshal your facts and draw the logical conclusions. This kind of behaviour will get us nowhere.

MEFF: As the actress said to the bishop.

DUST: Where's Rudge? Late. He was late last night.

He looks at his watch.

We were scheduled to begin five minutes ago.

MEFF: We 'ave, mate.

DUST: What?

MEFF: I've kicked off already. He's not written himself in for another ten minutes.

DUST: Every night the same excuse.

MEFF: You say that every night.

DUST: And you say that every night.

MEFF: And you say —

DUST: I'm not going to argue the point. I have a wife waiting for me, I trust this is realised.

MEFF: Every night you say —

DUST: *Exactly.* Night after night the same circular dialogue, round and round we go. You know what it's like? Do you know what it's like?

MEFF: It's like wading.

DUST: It's like wading — no, not wading; wading suggests being in it merely up to the thighs like a shrimp catcher — I am in it up to the armpits.

MEFF: Round and round . . .

DUST: Round and round the same nightmare municipal swimming bath, up to the armpits in —

MEFF: Not water.

DUST: — not water; water's clean, water you can see through, water rubs off, but mud, a kind of man-made imitation of primeval ooze . . . Meanwhile, my wife waits; we can't go to the cinema together . . . What does he expect to come out of this nightly rigmarole? Does he think one night we'll reach a conclusion? Doesn't he realise that it's always the same, that it can't be otherwise?

MEFF (*rolling a cigarette*): You want a roll, mate?

DUST: For the umpteenth time, no. Listen: you're a reasonable young man   no, you're not, but at least you're — uncommitted. Tell me — am I wrong? Can it be otherwise?

MEFF *lights his cigarette, ignoring him.*

Every night I ask the same question, every night he lights the same damned cigarette and gives me no answer. The same cigarette, mark you — I'll swear to it; the same shape, like a dog's hind leg, with an identical strand of cheap tobacco dangling out of the end. Watch the smoke come out through his nose.

MEFF *exhales through his nose.*

If he knew the Freudian implications behind that trick he'd think twice before doing it — not that he could help himself, he'd do it anyway. You don't understand how it can be the same cigarette. It's quite simple; it isn't really a cigarette at all, you see. It's the essence of cigarette; the artist's impression of cigarette, it isn't really there, you only think it is, and if you can think it's there today you can think it's there tomorrow. It's like Man — corruptible but recurrent. Just as a solid brass ashtray could rise of its own accord into the air if all its atoms happened to be going in the same direction at the same instant, so if everyone at once stopped thinking that cigarette existed, it no longer would.

Pause.

Don't bother to try. If there were a point, of course, all this would be beside it.

Pause. He throws his arms heavenwards

Will someone release me from my bondage?

Pause.

MEFF: No answer.

Pause.

DUST: The beginning is always the worst. The warming-up period. Later on one gets drawn into it in spite of oneself, one even imagines one is in control. Think of a steel ball rolling down a hill; faster and faster it goes, until its speed is enormous. Look at me, thinks the ball; I'm going as fast as I can. What power! Shall I try to go faster still? Shall I change direction? Shall I stop suddenly halfway down? I could if I wanted to, maybe in a moment I shall. It forgets gravity, you see. It forgets that even its mind is the mind of gravity, this foolish ball. That's how it will be later; when we've got up speed, when the juggernaut's taken over. The mahout will squat on top —

MEFF: Mahouts are for elephants . . .

DUST: — and imagine some mystical power is being transmitted through his bottom and the soles of his feet, to drive the monster along.

He sighs. Slight pause.

MEFF: Until that time.

DUST: Until that happy time I am a little god — grade two; I foresee every twist and turn of this sorry spectacle and can't do anything about it.

JAMES SAUNDERS

The pages which follow provide advice, in the form of Examiner's tips, on how to tackle the tasks set in the Exam practice section. Read the general points first before turning to the more specific advice given for each particular task.

General points

When the Board's examiners mark responses initially they work from descriptions of grades which represent various mark points. For instance, a Grade A performance, which represents a mark range of 19–25 out of 25, is described by UCLES in the following way:

'Essays at this highest level should show real originality and discrimination; candidates must prove they have responded vigorously to all or most of the key issues presented by the passage(s). They should have been able to identify, analyse and evaluate tone and attitude as well as argument and character; their handling of quotation and critical terms will have been assured, and their expression thoroughly fluent, economical and accurate.'

The description of Grade C, representing a mark range of 13–15, is as follows:

'These essays should show competent understanding and response; they may contain some evidence of qualities which, if sustained, would be worth a higher grade. Conscientious essays which pursue a thorough but rather unsophisticated argument are likely to fall within this grade. Expression has still to be accurate, but may lack some subtlety. Work which is distinctly promising but which lacks an adequate conclusion could receive marks in this range.'

The description of Grade E, representing a mark range of 7–9 out of 25, is as follows:

'Here candidates still have to show sound basic understanding of the texts and of how to respond to them, but analysis and evaluation will be limited and/or mechanical. There may be some misreadings, but not enough to undermine significantly the general ideas put forward. Expression may be hampered occasionally, but not seriously, by loss of clarity or accuracy. Work which shows promise but is seriously incomplete could appropriately receive marks in this range.'

It might also be useful to consider the following comments, which illustrate the examiner's approaches to assessment:

'Length does not equal quality. Some lengthy answers are thorough and interesting; others are repetitive and boring. Some brief answers are threadbare, others cogent and concise.'
' . . . the importance of the candidate's making an informed independent response . . . the candidate is the 'maker of meaning', you as examiner must evaluate what is offered without looking for what might have been presented or for what you might have written in the candidate's place!'

Task	Examiner's tip
1	With regard to this extract from *Wide Sargasso Sea*, you should note the narrative technique, the use of first person narrative, the creation of atmosphere, the use of dialogue and the creation of character. There is then the use of a story within a story and the movement between dream and reality. You should consider the use of song. You may well have read *Jane Eyre* or at least know the story and, if so, you should pick up the references to fire. Whether you have read it or not, however, you should — from the introduction and the tone of the extract — be able to pick up the idea of madness and see how it is hinted at in the extract.

Task	Examiner's tip

2   This is a very short text and you must show an awareness and understanding of each detail. You must express yourself with precision and clarity. You might find the poem a puzzle: it obviously has something to do with the structure and origin of words. Clearly the question, 'From where did the words arise?' is important and you must work out what the poet is saying about different kinds of words, both abstract and concrete. You should also examine in some detail the use of punctuation and the structure of the poem.

3   Both poems are about the ends of relationships and could be said to use similar approaches to their theme, but the Michael Drayton poem is a tightly structured sonnet whereas that by James Fenton is written in quatraines which use assonance rather than pure rhymes throughout. The simplicity of the repetitive final quatraine should be commented on, that simplicity being the end of love, and it should be contrasted with the personification in the final couplet of the sonnet, which holds out hope for recovery of the love.

4   In this extract relationships are explored: most importantly the relationship of Elizabeth with the rest of the family and her lack of comprehension of the father's behaviour and of the mother's and son's attitude to him. The climax of the extract — and it is a climax — is when the father takes control of the situation and the 'brutal' response of Elizabeth is because she realises that he has taken control. It is suggested that stage directions might be commented on, and they certainly enhance an understanding of the relationships. The style of the passage could almost be termed repartee, as there is only one speech of any length. Do not forget to comment on the humour of the Pennycuick story, part of its enjoyment being that it belongs to another age. It is important to keep at the forefront of your mind the fact that it is as a dramatic presentation which you are asked to explore.

5   In the examination proper, you have an hour to answer this question. It is a comparatively short poem and you are clearly expected to comment on it in considerable detail. Note that the question points you to the two experiences in the poem, picking a poppy and seeing a rat, and that you are asked to comment on theme, imagery, development of ideas, tone and use of language. The Flanders poppy very quickly became a symbol of death after the First World War; there is no disgust or hatred of the rat. In examining detail, look at the individual words, perhaps especially the adjectives in describing the rat, 'sardonic', 'droll', 'cosmopolitan', and in describing the place and the event, 'the sleeping green', 'the torn fields', 'shrieking iron', etc. In considering the poet's situation you should consider how the poem shows reflection and acceptance rather than anger and hate.

6   In some ways the wording of the question is extremely vague — 'You may write in whatever way you wish . . .' — but you are pointed very clearly to three considerations. You should consider that it is the opening of the novel and therefore has certain functions to perform. It introduces Edith Hope and it also creates an atmosphere. How you deal with these is up to you: you might start with the mood and the atmosphere of the place as this is what is so important in the first paragraph. Look at the vast grey lake: 'spreading like an anaesthetic towards the invisible further shore' and the way in which the contrast is made between the place in and out of season. Unless you know the novel, you can only speculate about Edith Hope's indiscretion which has led to her 'exile', but

Task	Examiner's tip

clearly it was in marked contrast to the ordinary common sense which is typified by the staccato sentences of the second paragraph. That introduction of place and central character would then lead you to consider the effectiveness of the extract as the opening of the novel. It does create atmosphere and character and raises questions which lead you to want to read on . . . .

7   *It Rains* has a very clear and personal memory at its centre, that of two lovers walking in the rain. In the first stanza there is an almost destructive force in the rain as it might potentially break down the vegetation. The hardness of the 'diamonds' of the rain are there. Those diamonds, however, become 'kisses' in the second stanza. The images then fade with the twilight and the loneliness. It is the structure of the second poem which is immediately noticeable, the long followed by the short rhyming line. The short line is virtually a throwaway, as each image of the picture after the rain is considered. Those different images create a mixture of a picture. The question asks you to consider diction, movement and emotional impact in comparing and contrasting the two poems. That is for you to decide — do not be afraid to express your view. If this writer finds more emotion in the first poem than the second, that does not necessarily mean you have to.

8   In the examination you have an hour in which to answer this question and the preamble rubric suggests you should spend a 'substantial proportion of your time reading the material and preparing and planning'. What is a 'substantial proportion'? We would suggest at least a third of the time available and possibly more. When an essay is fully and carefully planned, then the actual writing of the essay can take place at speed. Your starting point might be that the first poem uses a natural setting, whereas the second uses the desolation of the home and that both people are present in the Hardy whereas the one individual in the Duffy is alone, the second having gone. A key feature to explore is the use of imagery, and the use of apposite quotation is essential. Remember, as you explore, that you are not asked to arrive at a judgement.

9   You might well argue that the key to these passages is the relationship of the man to the city. Lively's man is in a situation where he is almost forced to explore the features of the city which surround him, whereas Ackroyd's man is trapped with his own fascination with what he knows about the area. In the first passage it is his irregular journey which produces the awareness of the mixed and varied features of the city, whereas in the second we are only pointed towards particular details, rather than a broad perspective. That may or may not be your way into your answer. Remember, whatever your approach, to explore ideas, language and style; use quotation and justify your interpretation of the passages.

10   There is an assumption in the question that the reader will share the writer's feelings of loss and affection and that assumption is probably correct. The affection is there in the central idea of the carousel ride which brings the poem full circle, and in the trivial detail: the 'striped pyjamas', 'the mint with the hole'. The loss is there in the religious metaphor,

> 'I have the ivory statues and the pictures
> telling stories of African ancestors,
> a birth, flights into Egypt.'

Task	Examiner's tip

It is also there in the central three-line section, 'How will I light the fire?' The poem is essentially quite simple and it is important that it is analysed in detail, factually, structurally and emotionally.

11   As so often in literature, here we have disturbance in life reflected by disturbance in nature. The storm and the agony go hand in hand with the death of the queen. Pericles' opening speech is a great mixture of prayer, fear, premonition and hope which needs to be analysed line by line to bring out its shifts in meaning. Look for the onomatopoeia and alliteration as the sound of the scene is conveyed. Dramatically, the baby is the centre of the confusion and overtakes both storm and tragedy. Examine the short speeches of Lychorida to see how she controls and calms with great care. It is important, as always with extracts from plays, to visualise as well as analyse.

12   What Eliot is considering in this essay is the role of Matthew Arnold as a literary critic who had the capacity to view literature from a completely new standpoint. Clearly, the opening sentence of the extract is of considerable importance: 'From time to time, every hundred years or so, it is desirable that some critic shall appear to review the past of our literature, and set the poets and the poems in a new order.' He reviews the 'master' critics and considers how the majority can only follow leads. He also considers the differences between eras. It is a short passage and you should consider each idea in detail; the ideas are expressed in an essentially straightforward way. The question then asks you to go further and to take the ideas and express your own view of the purpose of literary criticism. As always, you are not bound to follow the view of the writer but you are asked to stick closely to what he says and must not go off into flights of fancy.

13   Here we have an extract from a verse drama. You should consider the metre and rhythm of the lines as either contributing to, or inhibiting, the drama and reality of the situation. We have three clear speeches, and you should consider the content of each and how what is said provides an understanding of character and mood. Writing a commentary is fairly straightforward, in that you must work your way through the extract line by line, idea by idea, analysing and reacting. Perhaps a key word to react to in the second sentence is the word 'genuinely' as you might feel that there is almost a hidden agenda in the use of the word. As always, keep at the forefront of your mind that this is a play so, as well as being a great poem, it should also have a visual feel to it.

14   What is essential here is that you write in detail, as you are dealing with a fairly clear and straightforward passage. You are asked to look at character and situation and should consider all the individuals who are mentioned. For instance, although she is only peripheral, the Englishwoman has a clearly established character. What remains most important, however, is how Kumar reacts to the situation throughout.

Task	Examiner's tip

15 The question here is of a type which we have already explored several times, the instruction being to write a critical appreciation. This means that you must work your way through a process of analysis and evaluation, taking you to an expression of opinion. Your first decision, though, is which of the stimuli you are going to use as your basis. This is part of a three-hour paper and you have to answer three questions, this one being compulsory. Notionally, then, you have an hour. In this practice, spend some time carefully deciding which passage you would choose and then look back on the reasons for your choice. Decide if there are principles which you can apply to other questions of this type where you have this choice.

16 This is, in some ways, a similar task to the previous one. The first thing to do is to decide which stimulus you are going to respond to. Look back at the process you went through to make your previous decision and see whether you can apply the same principles as before. What is a little different here is that there are more pointers in the way in which the question is worded. Do, however, be aware of the words 'for example' in the second sentence of the question. A middle-range answer may well take each phrase of the sentence and develop ideas in response. The best answers will go beyond those ideas and develop personal ideas.

17 & 18 We have taken these tasks together because they introduce a new element to the task — associating the passages to the period to which they belong. They are taken from papers which centre around particular periods and it is therefore part of the study to have a concept of the period. You should look at theme, approach, vocabulary, structure etc. in your analysis. If you are not able to approach the passages from the period then substitute the common wording, 'Write an appreciation of the following passages'.

19 This question comes from a slightly different sort of paper from those we have used up till now. It is a paper entitled *Critical Explorations*. The first thing which must have struck you is that the quantity of material to be read is considerable. This is not making an outrageous demand in a time limited examination as the stimulus material is not only sent out in advance, but candidates are invited to annotate their copies, although it is carefully stipulated that no teacher intervention is allowed. The first thing to do, therefore, is just that — spend some time with the three extracts. These texts have not been chosen at random, but are the concluding paragraphs of each of the three novels. They therefore have a particular job to do for the writer — this is the last impression which characters, plot and writer will leave on the reader. In all your thinking concerning use of language, vocabulary and style, keep that very much at the forefront of your thinking. You might even make a special point of considering the final sentence of each extract.

From the wording of the first question, it is clear that the examiner believes that there are contrasts — both of writing and purpose — to be found. The second question implies that a powerful feeling will affect the reader's final view of characters. The third is asking the reader to consider the general atmosphere at the end of each novel and the feeling which will remain with the reader. These are clues to what needs to be explored in the passages.

Task	Examiner's tip

20
Again, remember that for the examination you would have been sent the material in advance and would have had a chance to annotate it — so take that chance now before you go any further.

At first glance the first question seems extraordinary — write about shoes! — but it is an important entry into the symbolism of the two plays, which is further pursued by the reference to seeming triviality in the third question.

Perhaps, as the questions possibly suggest, you will gain little from trying to analyse character in detail in these two extracts. What you must concentrate on here are the ideas and the form of the dialogue. Neither play is particularly straightforward to explain, there being little storyline or progression of plot. The use of what is close to repetition or a re-exploration of ideas is an important feature of the writing in each case.

If you are coming to these plays for the first time, keep firmly in mind that they are not trivial, but are probably two of the most important plays of the mid-twentieth century.

21
This poem comes from a section of the paper which is under the general title *Literature of Protest* and the question reflects this.

The first thing which must strike you about this poem is the violence of the images. They are intended to shock and do so:

'Mother-ant never surfaces
for father is enough meat, underground'

What also comes through very strongly is the contrast between the tradition of the native life and the changes brought about by progress. These are symbolised strongly by the red hills which have replaced the green hills of the past.

Analyse the poem carefully and be prepared to refer to and explain its effect on you as a reader.

22
Earlier in this book we used a passage from one of Ben Jonson's plays as the basis for one of our sample answers. This passage is from a rather less well known play of his, but the life of the characters and the situation is, in many ways, similar.

It is important to look at the stage direction and to visualise the bustle which surrounds this speech of Justice Overdo. There is a considerable amount of literary allusion in the speech, but there is also a structure which moves from one subject to another and one detail to another at a fairly breakneck speed.

Overdo is then overtaken by the fair people, who look forward to the later part of the day with optimism (more or less). It is important to analyse the interaction between the characters.

In your essay you should reflect on the pace and atmosphere which the dramatist is trying to create.

23
In the extract, Dust refers to 'circular dialogue' and in examining this dialogue, it is important that you keep this in mind. It is also important to note that there is a conscious awareness on the part of Meff and Dust that they are in a play and that there are performances night after night when the same thing happens in exactly the same way at exactly the same time.

Task　　　**Examiner's tip**

The situation which is being created is very artificial, you might argue, and the jokes are fairly excruciating, but this is probably deliberate and Meff knows how poor they are. They are used as another way of emphasising that this is a play as he brings the audience into the situation.

Having said that, it is important that you ask yourself the question: 'Is there a purpose in this dialogue — is there something behind the apparent triviality?'

This is the background to your essay.